"Your family business almost certainly has a culture, a set of understandings of 'who we are' and 'how we do things.' The question is, does your family's culture support family cohesiveness and business effectiveness? For a brilliant road map for getting the culture right, I recommend So You're in the Family Business. *It's lucidly written and full of compelling examples, and each chapter ends with bullet points for how to put into action the ideas you've just read."*

—Mitzi (Mrs. Frank) Perdue, author of *Tough Man, Tender Chicken: Business and Life Lessons from Frank Perdue*

"Based on many years of experience—together and individually—Paul and David Karofsky strike just the right balance between case studies and professional observations in their new book, So You're in the Family Business. *Written in their classic tongue-in-check, good-humored style, this book takes on the old, the new, and the inevitable challenges of owning and working in a family enterprise. Fun and useful, optimistic and realistic, serious but not too serious, it's a great contribution to the field."*

—Judy Green, PhD, president of Family Firm Institute

"This primer should be read by everyone who wants to learn best practices and avoid the pitfalls of a family business. The real-life client examples Paul and David share throughout the book are like having private access to decades of family business dos and don'ts."

—Craigie Zildjian, 14th generation CEO of The Zildjian Company

"I am deeply impressed by the Karofskys' encyclopedic knowledge about how family businesses work. As the longtime CEO of a fourth-generation family business, I have experienced their expertise firsthand and highly recommend this Guide to Sustainability to anyone who is interested in learning more about the challenges and opportunities facing family members who work together."

—Steve Grossman, former president and CEO of Grossman Marketing Group, former Massachusetts State Treasurer, and current CEO of Initiative for a Competitive Inner City (ICIC)

"Few things in life can be more rewarding and yet confusing as working in a family business. In this book, Paul and David provide a fantastic road map to realizing these rewards and clearing up the confusion. Their thinking has been an important element in our success through the years."

—McKeel Hagerty, CEO of Hagerty Group, YPO board chairman, 2016–2017

"Paul and David Karofsky demonstrate their vast experience and knowledge of family businesses in this informative and insightful book. Through a variety of case studies, they offer their individual perspectives and provide valuable guides to sustainability. They illustrate their deep understanding of the challenges unique to family businesses covering topics such as growing up in the family business, rules of engagement, family meetings, leadership, and ownership transition. A must-read for everyone involved in a family business."

—Debbie Lipsett, CEO (Chief Emotional Officer) of Charles River Apparel

"So You're in the Family Business provides practical help on many levels. At one level it offers good examples and bad examples. At a second level it provides possible interventions to improve outcomes. At the deepest level it will cause all participants in a potential family business career to engage in deep reflection on their own skills, interests, personalities, and time frames for measuring success. The family business can be a risky venture psychologically and financially for the ill-prepared. In this book, this father and son team provides both encouragement and warnings. It is a great service."

—Howard H. Stevenson, PhD, Sarofim-Rock Baker Foundation professor emeritus, former senior associate dean, director of publishing, and chair of the Harvard Business Publishing Company board

So You're in the Family Business...

So You're in the Family Business...

A Guide to Sustainability

Paul Karofsky & David Karofsky

Published by Advantage, Charleston, South Carolina.
Member of Advantage Media Group.

ADVANTAGE is a registered trademark, and the Advantage colophon is a trademark of Advantage Media Group, Inc.

Printed in the United States of America.

ISBN: 978-1-59932-749-5
LCCN: 2016952482

This publication is designed to provide accurate and authoritative information in regard to the subject matter covered. It is sold with the understanding that the publisher is not engaged in rendering legal, accounting, or other professional services. If legal advice or other expert assistance is required, the services of a competent professional person should be sought.

Advantage Media Group is proud to be a part of the Tree Neutral® program. Tree Neutral offsets the number of trees consumed in the production and printing of this book by taking proactive steps such as planting trees in direct proportion to the number of trees used to print books. To learn more about Tree Neutral, please visit **www.treeneutral.com.**

Table of Contents

■ ■ ■

Acknowledgments

■ ■ ■

To Lisa, my partner in life for fifty years, your love, support, and encouragement are boundless. You urged us to write this book before it was our dream. To our son, David, my partner and coauthor, whose innate understanding of people takes his grandfather's wisdom to a new level. To our daughter, Jody, whose compassion is a constant reminder of life's priorities. To our grandchildren, Adam, Syd, Matt, and Lily. You are our joy and inspiration. To my brother, Peter, whose constant support and whose love of medicine made my business entry seamless. "I am my brother's keeper. You are mine." To Jen and Larry, you are the daughter-in-law and son-in-law parents dream of. To the late Dr. Harry Levinson, our friend and mentor who encouraged us to stretch beyond our comfort zone. To the countless enterprising friends and families who teach us daily about the joys and challenges of working together. To our colleagues, whose shared wisdom has been invaluable. And to our editors, Jenny Tripp, Scott Neville, Lindsey Givens, Nate Best, Megan Elger, and the team at Advantage, whose guidance and attention to detail have made this process a pleasure.

—PAUL KAROFSKY

Acknowledgments

To Jen, my wife and best friend, you are truly the kindest, warmest person I have ever known. Your sense of family is incredible, and I am lucky to know you, let alone spend my life with you. To our son, Adam, your insight and inquisitiveness is astounding, along with your incredible work ethic. I admire you every day. To our daughter, Lily, your sense of loyalty to your friends and your amazing sense of humor bring light to our lives and those around you. Thank you for making me laugh. To my mother and father, Lisa and Paul, you are incredible parents who supported me through life's adventures and were always there to help guide me in the right direction and first showed me the true sense of the word "family." To my "big" sister, Jody, you have always been loving and caring, and I thank you for constantly being there for me. To my brothers and sisters-in-law and nieces and nephews, thank you for the support and love you have always provided. To my in-laws, Bob and Alba, I could not have asked for more loving, caring, and supportive in-laws. To my extended family and friends, thank you for making me laugh and for your encouragement through this exciting process.

—David Karofsky

Preface

■ ▨ ■

Our goal in writing this book is to whet your appetite for more—for you to join us in the journey as lifelong students of family enterprise and the quest for sustainability. The longer we work in this field and the more stories we hear of success and failure, the more we appreciate and marvel at the subtleties and intricacies of each. It's easy to simplify and generalize, but to do so devalues the incredible resources families bring forth and risks they take enduring sleepless nights in their mission to build careers of associates and produce goods and services for others, while shaping their own legacies. Each chapter of this book could be volumes unto itself. We simply want to share a glimpse into some of the challenges and opportunities we've faced with clients and in our own lives. You may wish to read this book cover to cover or perhaps scan the table of contents to explore the topic that interests you most at this moment in time. If you can walk away with some additional insights to better manage the dynamics and complexities of family enterprise, then we have accomplished our task. Statistically, the odds are stacked against us;[1] it's time to change those odds and create sustainable family enterprises that last longer than two or three generations. The stories we share are ones

---

1   Research conducted by Dr. Joseph Astrachan at Kennesaw University, a longtime expert in this field, concludes, "In each generation, it appears that approximately 30 percent of companies remain family owned."

that have been shared with us or are based on the clients with whom we've been privileged to work. Other than those of the Grossman and Zildjian families, whose mention is with their permission, these stories have been disguised out of respect for the families and businesses we so admire.

Introduction

■ ■ ■

"Tell me the truth. Are we the most dysfunctional family you've ever worked with?"

Almost invariably, that's one of the first questions we're asked when we're called in to consult with a family business. And yes, we have seen some spectacularly dysfunctional families in our practice, though few rise to the level of the fellow who pistol-whipped his own brother over a business dispute; the father who had an indiscreet relationship with his son's girlfriend; the mother who announced she was gay and leaving her husband and two adult sons to move in with her ex-sister-in-law; the father who said, "I'm not sure how happy I am with my son's success; look at what it says about what I couldn't do"; or the dad who struggled to give praise and, on his deathbed, told his son, "I don't want you to think I'm not proud of you." (The only way he could ultimately do it was with a double negative.)

Everybody hears the horror stories or sees the headlines about family businesses gone awry—yet, while there are numerous special challenges around running a family business, it doesn't have to be that way. The fact is, we are a family business, and for us it's been a wonderful experience. Through our consulting practice and family business peer groups, we work with business families to address challenges and opportunities ranging from communication and conflict resolution to defining roles and responsibilities to the transition of leadership and ownership.

Our mission is to help family members in business together enjoy Thanksgiving dinner with one another.

In this book, we'll share examples from our extensive practice in consulting to families whose relationships and enterprises were at risk, largely because of their failure to communicate effectively. In our experience, communication is the lynchpin for success, and improving communication among family members is the biggest part of our work. We hope you'll find our suggestions and the accompanying anecdotes both illuminating and inspiring.

If you are in a family business, we encourage you to think about the challenges and opportunities you may be facing in your own organization and ask yourself, *What changes can I make to have a more sustainable family enterprise?* We've developed a "Family Business Health Check," which may assist you in getting started. You can use this health check as a guide as you read through this book. It's located on our website at FamBizConsulting.com.

Chapter One

■ ▨ ■

Growing Up in the Family Business

Even though we're father and son partners in business together and both grew up in a family business, our paths to a shared enterprise were quite different. In this chapter, we'll share our individual, unique perspectives on what our past experiences meant and how they shaped our ideas about what a family business can and should be.

PAUL'S PERSPECTIVE

My dad was a second-generation son-in-law who gave up a promising career as an architect to help with our family's wallcovering business. When I was a youngster, on occasional Saturdays and school vacations, he'd take me to work with him. I savored it. I alphabetized metal plates with new customers' addresses and ran the Addressograph machine to print envelopes, folded and mailed invoices, and at month's end mailed statements, running them through the cranky Pitney Bowes postage meter. Price lists were printed with an A. B. Dick mimeograph machine. I'd check the ink supply and wrap the heavy, blue, wax paper stencil around the drum and insert long legal-size paper into the feeder. Blue was for retail stores and orange for sub-jobbers (retailers who inventoried for other retailers in their local markets). My challenge was to turn the crank slowly enough so ink would come through the holes in the stencils but not so slowly that it would blur the paper and yet not so fast that the paper would jam. Great fun, until, of course, it came to washing the ink off my hands. Typically, my fingers would have blue stains for a day or two afterward. I loved it. I loved working. I loved being with my dad, driving to work with him, having lunch with him, and seeing how he was respected and admired by his crew, who all called him "Syd" or "Mr. K." I felt an enormous sense of pride for this warm and engaging man and enjoyed the elevated privilege of calling him "Dad" or "Pop."

One of the greatest lessons I learned from my father was at the age of fifteen. I remember so clearly waking up that Sunday morning to find my mom standing in the front hall. She told me that there had been a massive fire in the middle of the night that destroyed our family's warehouse. My dad was there now. It was March 1, 1959. The headline of the *Boston Herald* read, "5-Alarm Roxbury Fire Rages." (See Addendum #1: *Boston Herald*.)

I dressed quickly, and Mom and I scrambled to the car. We couldn't park too close to the warehouse because the roads were gridlocked, so we cautiously walked a couple of ice-covered blocks to Washington Street. Water from the fire seemed to be everywhere. I'd never seen so many fire trucks, hook and ladders, hoses, and firefighters in one location. The smell of burned wallpaper permeated the crisp cold air. Smoke was pouring out of the black-streaked building.

My dad was standing across the street with a clipboard in one hand and a thick dark-green architectural pencil in the other. After some hugs, I asked him what he was doing. He said, "I'm planning."

"Planning what?" I replied.

He said, "Planning what to do next. I've got to call the mill in Ohio to order trailer loads of Wall-Tex."

"But where will they ship it?" I asked. "You don't have a warehouse anymore."

He said, "It will arrive next week. I'll have a new warehouse by then." No panic, no tears; this man was not obsessed with the tragedy that destroyed his warehouse. It didn't destroy his business. His business was his ideas and his team of incredibly devoted people. My dad was focused on the future opportunity and what needed to be done to rebuild, restock, and restore order to chaos.

Within two days, he found space at 300 Summer Street in Boston, just across Ft. Point Channel, the site of the Boston Tea Party. It was an old wool storage building owned and partially occupied by a furniture company. With eight stories and 108,000 square feet, the building was in the same block as one competitor and a block away from two others. It was a building we'd ultimately purchase (see Addendum #2: Summer Street). Dad arranged to rent four floors, just enough to handle the present size of the business and allow for some growth. The space was totally bare, with reinforced concrete floors capable of holding heavy loads. Two freight elevators and a ground floor rear alley were perfect for a chute to the street for customer pick-ups. Contractors, electricians, even the telephone company responded immediately to my dad's urgent pleas for help. And within ten days he was back in business and at the end of the month hosted an open house party for his crew, customers, suppliers, and even all the contractors who helped him rebuild.

FLASH BACKWARD: PAUL'S STORY

One of the greatest gifts my mother gave me as a young child was her counsel, "You can't have your cake and eat it too." From the moment I heard that, I was determined to prove her wrong.

This was evidenced with great clarity when I was a junior in high school. I was preparing for a Spanish speaking contest, and my teacher asked if I'd mind coming to his home on a Saturday for some additional help. I was stunned when I arrived at a stately Georgian colonial with cream-colored pillars and a front door of wrought iron and glass. When my teacher opened the door, my first question was, "You weren't always a teacher were you?" He laughed and then told me that his first career in business was rewarding, but he, as have I, had always wanted to be a teacher. So, after an early retirement, he returned to school and earned a graduate degree in foreign languages and had been teaching ever since. Several years later, I learned of a family friend who opted out of his family's business also to return to school, earned his doctorate, and devoted his second career to helping others in the field of social work.

At a pre-conscious level, a path was forming where I could have my cake and eat it too.

After my undergraduate years, now a newlywed, I attended graduate school in philosophy while my bride completed her under-graduate studies. I was the only graduate student in the department, and part of my responsibility included working as a teaching assistant in an introductory undergraduate course. My professor was officious, shallow, cold, curt, and insensitive. Most of my students were taking the course as a distribution requirement, with little interest in the subject. I had no peers, and there was no room to share my own thoughts and ideas. My disappointment and disillusionment, perhaps a token of my relative youth and naiveté, led me to abandon my studies halfway through. I then became a substitute teacher in local high schools, coupled with part-time work in a hardware store, selling paint, wallpaper, and salt lick. I loved both of my new careers; I had my cake and could eat it too. But I knew this was a short-term event. We were in Connecticut, and my wife and I wanted to live closer to our families in the Boston area.

The following year, I joined my dad in the wholesale distribution side of our family's wallcovering business (more to follow). My uncle, his cousin, my grandmother, and her second husband ran the retail end. Shortly after my entry, my dad, anticipating the complexities of family enterprise, arranged a buy-out to separate the wholesale from retail to assure our independence. My role and responsibility steadily grew, and we opened a branch distribution center in Connecticut and made a couple of major acquisitions (more on this later), increasing the business more than tenfold over a ten-year period.

While I enjoyed the strategic aspects of business, the trappings of success, and the joy of a growing family with two spectacular kids, I needed more. I needed some cake again.

I read a book by another family friend entitled *Second Time Around: An Alternative to Retirement* and was freshly inspired. I joined a local nighttime hotline telephone support for teens in trouble, then a local multiservice center for drop-ins. Later, for twelve years, while still active in our family's business, I co-taught a nighttime course in human relations at our local high school. The cake tasted good.

The frosting came several years later when our industry hit a peak and I opted to sell our business, which my dad had earlier transitioned to me. Encouraged by a psychiatrist friend, I returned to graduate school and focused on the psychosocial lives of families and intergenerational relationships.

Now in my midforties, armed with a new piece of parchment and encouraged by a cousin who was launching his second career in the world of strategic philanthropy, I learned that the world of family business was emerging as a discipline. Seeking opportunities in local universities, I discovered that Northeastern University was exploring the launch of a Center for Family Business. I was invited to consult on that launch, became its executive director, and ran the center with great success, producing monthly breakfast meetings and bimonthly half-day educational forums with guest speakers. I also had the joy of creating and facilitating a series of peer forums: two leadership development forums, a seniors' forum, an intergenerational forum, and a women's forum.

At its peak, the center had seventy-five families and six professional sponsors participating in a learning community. Together we explored the challenges and opportunities of family enterprise, ranging from succession, roles and responsibilities, and taking hold and letting go, to conflict management, while over the fourteen years achieving a revenue surplus of over $500,000 for the Dean's Discretionary Fund. During this time, I was asked to speak, write, teach, and consult to business families; launched Transition Consulting Group; and savored a worldwide speaking tour with the Young Presidents' Organization.

The frosting got sweeter when I retired from the center and my son, David, joined me in consulting to business families. Armed with his master's degree in counseling psychology, an MBA, twenty years of work experience, and an innately irreplaceable sense of people, he was duly qualified.

Today, as a family business working with other family businesses, we share the frosting as partners and father and son as we speak, write, teach, and consult with family enterprises and facilitate multiple peer forums through The Peer Alliance. And just as I was able to make changes in our family business, be my own person, and take it in a direction that was different than what my dad had originally started, so David has taken our business to a new level and changed it, and will continue to change it, in many ways as he applies his own unique skill set. I'm thoroughly comfortable embracing these changes. The future is his.

DAVID'S PERSPECTIVE

Going back to the early 1900s, family business has been a way of life for our family, something that's in our blood, my dad being the third generation in our family's wholesale wallcovering business. Although the nature of our family business itself has changed, the work that we do today and the experiences that we have today with each other and with our clients are a result of having been in a family enterprise for four generations.

From the time I was about seven to when I was seventeen, every quarter my father would send a company newsletter to key customers, suppliers, and other vendors, about a thousand letters altogether, although to me it felt more like ten thousand. He'd bring them home, pop them on the dining room table, and say, "All right. Here's your weekend." We would sit next to each other. He'd have a stack of letters and personally sign each one. I would then fold them and put them in envelopes. By Sunday afternoon, we had boxes of envelopes ready to be mailed. It felt like I was contributing to the family enterprise, that I was doing something meaningful, even when I was very young. I would read the letters so I was learning what my father and grandfather were saying to their customers, and I got a sense of what was going on in the business. I was a little bit a part of it, which felt great.

When I had vacations in grade school, Dad would bring me to work with him in Boston. The building was downtown on Summer Street, and my father and grandfather's offices were there right next to each other, with a small private door between them. Dad had a big office with a couch and a round table with four or five chairs around it and a desk and credenza. Best of all, he had a closet filled with what looked like all the office supplies in the world. As a ten-year-old kid, I thought that was the coolest thing in the world.

One thing I loved in particular was a small Lucite note holder my dad had on his desk that held two-by-two-inch notes with his initials on them. He used to bring me stacks of those, and I'd change the initials on them to mine. When I saved up enough money, I went to the stationers and bought my own.

When I was in the office on school vacations, I would go down to what we called "the bat cave" where all the samples and all the wallpaper were warehoused. Together with an employee named Carl, I would cut sample books. We had to wear heavy overcoats to protect our clothes from the ink. After cutting the sample books, I would go upstairs, and my father, grandfather, and I would walk down the street to Lodge's Diner. We would talk about business and life, and I felt like one of the guys. I played on the company softball team, and I remember the uniform: a blue-and-white striped shirt with an arrow insignia on the chest and a hat with the Northeastern arrow on it. I was a boy among men, but I remember standing at the plate and taking my swings, and it was a lot of fun. Family business was more than an enterprise to earn money. It was a way of life. It was our way of life, three generations working together. We knew nothing different. Even on Sundays, the whole family, including both sets of grandparents, went to dinner together.

We first talked about my joining my father in business when I was thirty years old. Married, with a young son, I was finishing up my MBA and in the middle of my internship working for a Fortune 500 company. My father has always been the person I would talk to and bounce ideas off of. We were having dinner when he asked me, "Well, what's next?"

I said, "I'm not sure what I want to do. It would it be fun if you and I did something." He agreed it would be great, and after exploring the pros and cons he suggested that at age thirty, I'd need to get a PhD. I already had a master's in counseling psychology and was working on my second master's, and frankly, the last thing I wanted to do was go back to school. I wanted to get out into the workplace and start earning for my family, so we put the idea on the back burner and both said, "Well, maybe one day." I went off and had a career of my own in high tech and did a lot of different things, from working at EMC to running marketing for a software start-up—and gathering that essential nonfamily-business work experience.

The door opened again at age thirty-nine when I had the work experience and the maturity to be an effective contributor to the family business and to really be a good family business consultant (more about this in chapter 2).

For seventeen years, Transition Consulting Group was not a family business. It was my dad consulting, doing his own thing, working with clients as he wanted to. Then, all of a sudden, the dynamic changed when I came in. I think one of the best things about it for my father was that it brought his family business experience full circle. Now he is the senior generation, and that's a rich and rewarding life experience for him as well as for me (more about this to follow).

GUIDELINES FOR SUSTAINABILITY

- Challenges are inevitable; learn to manage them.
- Recognize that you are your children's mirror.
- Model the attitude and behaviors you'd like to see endure.
- Provide your kids with positive experiences in the business.

- Engage them early on; make it fun.

- Focus on solutions, not problems.

- Share stories and find opportunities to instill values.

- Recognize your passion. Maybe you can have your cake and eat it too.

- Sometimes it's okay for the business to serve the family; a sale can enable that.

- Ensure that each generation brings and applies unique skill sets; embrace them.

- Nurture the interest and excitement of the next generation.

- Keep the door open. What might not work today may just be perfect tomorrow.

Chapter Two

■ ■ ■

The Rules of Engagement: Why You Need to Establish Entry Criteria

When is the best time to write a prenuptial agreement? Hint: it's not the day before the wedding—much less the day after. Just as you would create rules before playing a game of basketball or baseball, we encourage you to create rules in the family business. Defined entry criteria for family members—what we call *The Rules of Engagement*— are the business equivalent of prenups, or rules in a game, and should be spelled out, agreed upon, and in place well in advance of need. They're more than requirements for education and outside work experience. Failure to establish and adhere to these rules is typically an invitation to disaster.

There are two client stories that instantly come to mind that provide real-life illustrations of how things can go very wrong, or very right, depending on how thoughtfully this process is managed.

HOW IT LOOKS WHEN YOU DO THINGS INCORRECTLY

Let's start with the train wreck. The DeLeon family owned a chain of successful, high-end restaurants, which were jointly run by two sisters and their brother. It was a silo-mentality organization—in that each of the three siblings was focused on running his or her specific department—and there were already fault lines in the family relationships, thanks to differing opinions on the vision for the business and the varying levels of strength in the siblings' capabilities to run their respective operations.

One of the sisters, Martina, had a ne'er-do-well son, Chuck, who had just barely graduated from college and didn't have a clue about what he wanted to do. He'd spent some summers and weekends working in the business, but he hadn't put much effort into it, typically showing up late and leaving early. His passion in college had been basketball, but he wasn't NBA material, so he came to his mother and asked her for a job. Her response? "Sure, come on board. We'll figure it out." No entry criteria, no past experience, inadequate education, no established rules on what his role was going to be or to whom he was going to report; he just showed up for work, driving the shiny new BMW his mom had bought him as a graduation gift.

Not surprisingly, what ensued were conflict, animosity, and a further fracturing of family relationships. Martina's brother and sister didn't want to tell her that Chuck wasn't the brightest bulb, but it was clear he had little to nothing to contribute. And that $80K Beemer didn't endear him to his coworkers, who were only too ready to write off the boss's kid as an entitled brat. This further clouded the siblings' sense of vision, and a fairly smooth-running business was suddenly plunged into drama; nobody was communicating, and resentments were at the boiling point when we were called in to help salvage the situation.

We facilitated discussion to create a training rotation where Chuck would spend three months in different areas of the business: working in the kitchens; waiting tables; working in management, finance, and operations, etc., to learn the business from the ground up. But a lot of damage had already been done. Chuck had been reporting to his uncle, who gave him a series of "special assignments," none of which was performed well or on time. This was exacerbated by Chuck's obvious sense of entitlement; Celtics games were his priority, so forget working night shifts when the team was in town. Despite this, his uncle was unable to give constructive feedback for fear it would further exacerbate tension between him and his sister. The consequence: ensuing friction threatened to derail the business.

We sat down with all the principals, including Chuck, and led a frank conversation. We guided the siblings to lay the issues out with complete, yet respectful, candor because it was important that all understood that Chuck had been set up for failure the day he was hired, that his behavior had been unacceptable, and that many of his problems were of his own making. At that point, everyone realized that for Chuck to get the respect he wanted (and the company needed), he'd have to leave the company and prove himself outside his family's business. Ultimately, the three siblings were able to repair their relationships with more open and candid dialogue, and Chuck is now working successfully for another company. In effect, we helped the family reverse-engineer their rules of engagement and entry criteria, and while it came too late for Chuck, the process and guidelines they created are serving them now in smoothing the entrance of other next-gens to the family business.

HOW IT LOOKS WHEN YOU DO THINGS CORRECTLY

A good example of doing things right is the story of Hank and his son, Chad. Hank had divorced his wife soon after their son was born, and Chad was raised two states away from his dad. As a consequence, their relationship during Chad's childhood was spotty at best, something Hank regretted enormously. Hank had inherited a large manufacturing facility and built the business into one of the premiere companies of its kind in the country. Meanwhile, Chad took his own route, going to college and earning a law degree. After Chad worked in a law firm for three years plus four more as corporate counsel in a related field, his dad, wanting to craft a plan for succession and hoping that his son might ultimately take over, invited Chad to join the business. Chad agreed, seeing this as a wonderful opportunity for his own career, as well as a chance to build the relationship he'd always wanted with his dad.

Both Chad and Hank understood the risks of bringing a member of the younger generation into the business, so we were hired to perform due diligence for Chad's entry. This involved in-depth interviews with both father and son to establish clarity around several critical questions: What were their goals? What were their expectations for the future? What kind of a vision did each of them have? What were their tolerances for risk, and were those well matched? We checked for compatibility of personality and style. We performed an in-depth assessment of Chad's competencies, along with multiple interviews of key stakeholders in the business: nonfamily employees, the company's attorney, the company's banker, and other important players.

Through this process, we determined that Chad did, in fact, have the competencies required to ultimately run his father's business. He entered at a high level, and it worked out beautifully. Father and son went on to make major acquisitions and build on Hank's successes— and to patch up that long-neglected father–son relationship.

MANAGING EXPECTATIONS IS KEY

Managing expectations is a key factor in all of this, on both ends, and the family members must be proactive rather than reactive.

When expectations are not properly managed, conflict ensues. If the member of the younger generation coming aboard understands what's required and can perform up to the expectations of senior management, of other family members, and of the rest of the company, then things run more smoothly.

SUGGESTED RULES OF ENGAGEMENT

There are lots of broad issues—education, experience, and skills—and, of course, the essentials of personality and style. But there's no single right answer. The right answer is what works for the family. We've worked with families that have had strict and specific entry criteria: a specific level of education, a minimum number of years working outside the business, compensation at fair market value, and the expectation that next-gens will come in at an entry level. Others are comfortable with less-stringent requirements. These guidelines can't be written in cement; times change and standards with them, and different businesses have different needs. Even those families with the most rigid criteria typically reevaluate them as each new generation comes in. A fourth-generation family business will likely have vastly different rules of engagement than it did a generation or two before.

One other piece that's often overlooked, but which we find vitally important, is exploring with next-generation family members their reasons for wanting to come aboard. Are they joining out of a passion and love for the business? Are they hoping to rebuild a damaged relationship with a parent or because they can't find any other job and this is a default solution? Whatever is driving their choice, it is absolutely necessary to have an open family discussion about it.

Bottom line, it's important to recognize that entry to the family business is not a given. These aren't nineteenth-century family farms we're talking about, and kids today are less likely than they were in previous generations to have literally "grown up" working for the family firm. Joining the family business today is a matter of choice, not of obligation, and certainly is not an entitlement.

PAUL'S PERSPECTIVE

As I mentioned in chapter 1, I was married when I left graduate school; I knew I needed to support my wife, so I got a job selling paint, wallpaper, and salt lick in a local hardware store and worked as a substitute teacher. It was clear that teaching wouldn't afford me the lifestyle I wanted, and working in a retail store wasn't much of a challenge, so I approached my dad and told him that I wanted to explore the potential of a future with the family business. He said, "Come on up to Boston, and we'll talk." That was in the spring of 1967.

I vividly remember sitting across from him at his desk. He was telling me stories about the history of the company, many of which I knew, and also about his vision for the future, which I'd never really heard before—his desire for growth and training a leader for the next generation. I told him I'd like to be part of this company. He surprised me by asking, "How do you know it's any good?"

I said, "What do you mean?"

"How do you know it makes financial sense for you and your future?"

"We always lived comfortably, so I figured it was okay."

"Well, you took an accounting course in college. Why don't you take these books and go through them?" He opened a drawer and pulled out twenty blue books, the year-end financial statements for the first twenty years of the distribution business. He handed them to me, along with a large unfolding paper graph that he had kept from the day he'd started. On it, he'd tracked monthly sales for the first couple of years, then quarterly sales for the next few years, and finally annual sales growth and profitability.

I took those blue books with me into another room and came back to his office an hour later.

"Dad, from my limited perspective, it sure looks like a healthy business. Steady growth, no debt, consistent reinvestment, seems like a great opportunity. But I have a question."

He said, "Shoot."

"This loan on the books to officers—is that how you put me through college and my brother through medical school?"

He said, "Yes. Good catch. I'm proud of you for seeing that. What do you think?"

"Dad, I would absolutely love to work for you."

He looked at me with a serious expression and said, "Paul, you will never work *for* me one day in your life, but you can work *with* me." That set the tone for our working relationship; he never wanted me to have the feeling of being subordinate to him but rather that I was his partner.

We had no entry criteria; they didn't exist then. While I certainly don't recommend that for today's businesses, it worked for us. In many ways, I was just lucky; the foundational relationship with my dad was solid, our communication was good, I had the education, and there was a need and an opportunity for me there. I had worked there during the summers, and I knew what the business was about. Most importantly, I had the trust and the respect of others in the organization. I came in at $150/week, reporting to the general manager, with no title, and worked in the order department, which was the heart and soul of the business and also had a small sales territory. After a year or two, I got involved in the financial aspects of the business, overseeing collections, doing accounts receivable and making collection calls, and developing a budgeting process. I joined my dad in meetings with the bank, insurance company, and attorney and ultimately got an office and became vice president, executive vice president, and ultimately president and CEO as I assumed more and more responsibility.

When David and I decided that we would work together in business, I wanted to follow my dad's model and likewise never have David feel he was working *for* me, so I took the corporation that I had started twenty years earlier and dissolved it, and we started a new corporation together as equal partners. We had clarity on roles and responsibilities. We had clarity on compensation. We had clarity on a buy–sell agreement. We put in place all the practices that we try to encourage for our clients, so we'd be living what we were teaching.

DAVID'S PERSPECTIVE

I entered this family business in a markedly different manner from my father. When I was in grad school getting my MBA, we had talked about me coming into the business and what that might look like. We both agreed that the timing just wasn't right for me or for the business, so I went off and had a highly successful career in several areas, building my résumé and experience.

Fast-forward to ten years later, 2009; I was now thirty-nine, wrapping up a role with a start-up company and looking for a new opportunity. That's when Dad and I circled back to discuss starting something new together. There were few, if any, other father–son teams consulting to family businesses, which gave us the opportunity to immediately differentiate ourselves.

Dad and I had an initial telephone conversation when I put forward the idea of working together. It was a thought we both had at the same time and a conversation that ended with us agreeing to discuss it further. I know my dad; he's a deep fact-finder who likes to do extensive research and lay things out, and I knew he'd be doing that before we spoke again. I was in Orlando on a business trip when he came up to spend the day with me to talk about it. We were sitting outside at a café, and I remember that he asked me to take off my sunglasses. When I asked him why, he told me, "I want to see your eyes when we talk because your eyes speak volumes."

I took them off, and we went on to have a substantive conversation about how to proceed, if we chose to do so: what's the timing, what are the roles, and what would this partnership look like? Primarily, it was Dad asking me for my thoughts; he was more interested in hearing what I wanted and about my vision than anything else because he knew that if we were to do this, it would be our company but my future. For him, the commitment might be ten to fifteen years, but for me, it was a thirty-year play, so we each needed to understand where the other was coming from and what our motivations were. (As it turned out, one of the biggest takeaways from that trip for me was never to share a hotel room with my dad again; his snoring was so earsplitting that even a pair of high-end noise-cancelling headphones didn't block it out!) That's when we began the process of laying the foundation for what the rest of our business relationship would look like.

I went home to discuss it with my wife; Dad agreed to talk it over with Mom. We continued the conversation in greater detail, exploring what I would need to do to get ready to get into the consulting side. Both of us called my sister, Jody, to tell her what we were considering; she thought it was great and gave us her blessing. Our next big discussion happened over Thanksgiving weekend, when my folks came to our house for the holiday. The four of us—my father, my mother, my wife, and I—sat down to talk about it. That's when Dad and I laid out the plan, everything from where we would work and the roles we would have to how ownership was structured. We needed and wanted my mom's and wife's unequivocal support, and we got it.

With a master's in counseling psychology, an MBA, twenty years of varied business experience, and soon to obtain certificates in family business and family wealth advising, I felt confident that with a competent mentor I'd continue learning and feel comfortable facilitating, coaching, and guiding family business discussions. Subsequently, we met with our accountant, who helped us think through what kind of financial entity we'd be creating. We met with an attorney and settled on a structure for our new corporation and created a buy–sell agreement. One of the most meaningful gestures was something my dad did for me; he took the stock certificate you get when you start a new company, with both of our signatures on it, had it etched on glass and presented it to me. (See Addendum #3: Etched Stock Certificate.) That was his way of saying, "You'll never work *for* me; you'll work *with* me," of cementing that mantra into our family culture. If my son or daughter comes into the business, they'll never work for me a day in their lives; they will work with me.

GUIDELINES FOR SUSTAINABILITY

- Set rules of engagement and entry criteria well in advance to keep them objective and not focused on one new entrant.

- Assess the suitability of entry with as much objectivity as possible.

- Recognize that younger generation family members will be under a microscope. A new BMW is not the best "signing bonus."

- Consider assessing the competencies of the next generation.

- Make sure the next generation doesn't come in with a sense of entitlement; that will spark hostility in the workplace.

- Clearly spell out compensation, benefits, and vacation time, in line with what is given to nonfamily employees.

- Allow the next generation family members to learn new skills and to make their rookie mistakes elsewhere via prior work experience, which provides an understanding of the job search and hiring process. It also ensures they'll work for a boss with objectivity. Most importantly, it allows them to prove themselves, to see that they have value in the marketplace as capable, independent individuals who are not dependent on the family enterprise for survival. This proof of competence and the confidence it creates can't be gained in any other way. It's also critical for the parent who may at some point consider selling the business but must balance that choice against his fears that his kids can't make it on their own.

- Understand the reason for entry. Is it a passion for the business? Is it a default position because no other job is available? Is it an attempt to repair a relationship? The latter two might be components but ought not be the driving forces.

- Be sure younger family members report to a nonfamily member whenever possible to ensure (to the greatest extent possible) more objective feedback.

- Consider starting your new family employees out in a rotation through your various departments. Rotating through different positions in the company provides a much fuller understanding of how the whole business works and (when done well) gains the respect and appreciation of nonfamily employees. This is especially important for smaller companies.

- Clarify rules of engagement, and provide specific, expected behaviors. Explain the track to management. If leading to a senior position, in addition to the typical qualifications of knowledge, skill, experience, attitude, and style, ensure alignment on risk tolerance, growth, and vision.

- Ensure your children don't work *for* you but instead work *with* you.

- Have conversations about the family business early and often with your next-generation leaders. Make sure they understand your culture, your values, and your expectations, from attitude to work ethic and more.

Chapter Three

■ ▧ ■

Roles and Responsibilities

When we ask family members in business together what they do, the response is frequently a rather glib, "Whatever needs to be done." That's what entrepreneurs do when they start a business. But as the business grows and matures, especially through multiple generations, the need for structure, clarity, and agreement around who does what and who reports to whom is vital for maintaining harmony in both the family and the family business. Sometimes there's an open position in the business, and a family member fits the bill. Other times, a position is created for a family member based on his or her knowledge, skill, and experience. And we've seen family members paid more than a million dollars a year to stay home. Businesses and family relationships can be significantly damaged if it's not clear to everyone where people stand and what's expected of them.

There's more to determining appropriate roles than simply weighing competencies. All too often, when assigning positions in the business, we see too much focus on industry and task knowledge without enough attention being given to style, personality, attitude, and the needs of the business. Inappropriate assignment and/or misunderstanding regarding roles and responsibilities is a prescription for discord and confusion within a family business, and the stories that follow about families with whom we've worked illustrate how badly things can go when confusion reigns.

A LACK OF ROLE CLARITY
LEADS TO RESENTMENT

Let's begin with the Ferrand family. The youngest son, Richard, was a truly independent soul. He marched to his own drum and never liked taking orders from anyone, as a child or as an adult. He hoped for a major league baseball career, but an injury permanently quashed that ambition and left him rudderless after college. Rich had a sweet and engaging personality and had always been his dad's favorite. It wasn't surprising that his siblings resented him, as he had been spoiled and pampered since he was born—and his entry into the family business was no different. His sister, Sarah, who managed the business, thought he reported to her. But he thought he reported to his father, the chairman of the board. With no entry criteria and no job description, he was simply assigned a desk and put on salary, with a vague assignment for "staff relations." He'd show up in a suit and a tie, looking every inch a corporate executive, but never got anything done.

When he did try and assert himself in one particular instance at an important meeting, it was a disaster; he lacked the background and basic knowledge required to represent the company and offered promises and commitments that he had neither the expertise nor the authority to make. Frankly, had he not been a family member, he would have been on the street that afternoon. His coworkers, who saw him in action that day, were astonished to hear him make assurances on behalf of the business when they knew the potential repercussions could be disastrous. It was clear to everyone that he was completely overstepping his bounds, a real loose cannon.

We were initially called in by Sarah, who had heard us speak at a family business conference. His mom and dad had insisted that Rich have a job, but his sister didn't know how to handle the problems he was creating, and it was generating massive conflict among them all. The parents didn't want to hurt Rich's feelings by addressing his incompetence directly, which put Sarah in a highly compromised position. In effect, the parents were exacerbating the problem by refusing to acknowledge that there was one.

We began by meeting with the whole family together to break the situation down into its individual parts and create family goals for the engagement. Subsequently, we suggested that Rich get some feedback on his job performance. Not surprisingly, he flatly refused to participate in a performance appraisal process, probably because he was terrified of the results. Yet he needed feedback to understand how others perceived his behavior. Absent parental authority and Rich's heightened self-awareness, there would be no change. The ultimate consequence in a business is getting fired if you don't perform. Without that ultimate consequence, Rich could do whatever he wanted since he knew his parents wouldn't allow his sister to fire him.

The most important work we did was with the parents by helping them to understand the impact of their actions (or, rather, their inaction) on Rich and Sarah—his self-esteem and her relationship with her brother—plus the fallout with the rest of their staff. Mom and Dad needed to empower Sarah as Rich's "boss." The parents had to be coached on how to help Rich understand that his actions had consequences and that he was accountable to himself and the organization at large. Once the parents were on board, we were able to help the family find a clearly defined role for Rich that made sense in the business, one that matched both the business's needs and his capabilities.

A LACK OF CLARITY OF ROLES LEADS TO CONFUSION

Another example of a family business that was floundering over a lack of clear roles and responsibilities presented a markedly different dynamic. The father at the head of the Garibaldi family business ran it like a virtual dictatorship, as had his own father and grandfather. After initial interviews with Dad and his children in the business, Dad called us into his office and asked what we thought. We candidly and respectfully replied, "Your kids think you're pretty tough."

"Tough?" he bellowed, smashing his fist on his desk. "Tough, tough? How can they say I'm tough? I never, ever hit any of my kids!" The kids (three sons in their fifties) had spent their summers working at the business but came in with neither defined roles nor clear responsibilities. Feelings were consistently denied. Now a fourth-generation family business, their motto might as well have been, "I don't care what you feel, just suck it up and get your job done," with a couple of choice four-letter words thrown in for emphasis. The family seldom met as a group to talk about priorities; there was minimal to no communication among the family members, no effective process for decision making, no plan for sustainability, and no tender feelings. Hostility, bickering, and profane name-calling were the standard.

When the sons contacted us, they presented us with a two-pronged challenge to receive their father's support: first was achieving clarity on their roles and second was gaining alignment with each other regarding the future. Their unclear roles and responsibilities stymied decision making in the company by anyone other than their father, who was now in his seventies and experiencing some health issues. When a family business has been run the way he'd been running it—making every decision, controlling every component of the business—and the strongman at the helm shows signs of faltering in his abilities, it causes a tremendous amount of fear in the company because everyone is suddenly aware that there is no structure in place for the sustainability of the business. The three sons wanted to have this discussion independent of their father because they felt the issues were more about the three of them than about him, which was only *partly* true.

When we met with the brothers, it was quickly clear to us that a big part of their conflict sprang from the fact that not one of them knew what he was supposed to be doing day in and day out, nor did any one of them know what each of his brothers did. When we spoke to their father, we learned that despite his awareness of the problem, he was unsure how to fix it. His response was, "My sons have to figure it out on their own." And until they did, Dad wasn't going to grant them any meaningful roles or decision-making powers.

The second part of the challenge required helping the three brothers find common ground and align on key issues. These included their vision for the future of the business, how they wanted to work together, and what roles each of them should have in the organization, now and in the future, that would allow them to personally and collectively succeed while also meeting the needs of the business. This, of course, required creating a vision, goal setting, and strategic planning to understand where the business has been and where the principals want to see it headed.

COMMUNICATION IS THE BOTTOM LINE

So much of this process was building a foundation and process for communication among the siblings so they could unravel not only the personal conflicts they had with one another but also gain appreciation for the strengths and the skills each one brought to the table. Their mutual hostility, their resentment of one another, and their frustration with one another all went back to a code of silence, misperceptions, and borderline abusively negative feedback with which this family was raised, one that ran multiple generations deep. A major culture shift was required in order to break through it.

HOW CAN THIS KIND OF SCENARIO BE PREVENTED?

It begins with creating a culture of open communication among family members, one that acknowledges that it's okay to have feelings and to talk about them and that feelings can't be denied. We can't simply shut people down by saying, "You shouldn't feel that way." People feel the way they feel; the strength of the family comes through accepting people for who they are, along with having transparency and openness in talking about it.

Ultimately, with the added help from our referral to a family therapist, the Garibaldi brothers were able to address the dynamics among them and gained the ability to have open and candid conversations with one another. We worked with them to present a plan to their father with clarity on roles and responsibilities for each. Dad accepted the plan; all he ever wanted was for them to get along with one another and figure out how to work together.

A third example is Royal Capital, a rapidly growing telecommunication business now in its second generation. Its success is clearly due to the work of the founder and CEO, Harold, under whose hand the business has grown exponentially. His son-in-law, Steven, a CPA, joined the company ten years previously, immediately after his marriage to Harold's only child. He was positioned as the chief financial officer and was seen as the presumptive heir.

Much of Harold's achievement was attributable to his management style: generous in granting authority and responsibility to others and with a culture of giving people the benefit of the doubt—but with a twist. Support and trust were granted to others who were picked and promoted based on how well their views and ideas aligned with Harold's. So long as people didn't rock the boat or try to steer it in a direction Harold didn't like, their jobs were safe. It was Harold's way or the highway: the iron fist in the velvet glove.

Like his father-in-law, Steven cared deeply about the business but was the only one willing to push back against Harold's benevolent dictatorship. He wasn't just going to roll over and kowtow to his father-in-law, so he challenged the status quo, albeit not always in the most respectful way: Harold would make suggestions, and then Steven would confront him and ask for more data. The other executive leaders didn't understand his quest for more information, for clarity and accuracy, and felt that Steven was disrespectful and insufficiently appreciative of Harold. They frankly viewed him as an entitled jerk with a negatively stereotypical accountant's mentality.

Steven's analytical approach was his way of seeking to create greater accountability, but the staff saw it as an open challenge to Harold. The tension between Steven and Harold naturally created strife, and Harold discontinued semi-annual family travel. Steven was perceived as the antagonist, when in reality he was more often the victim. He was highly focused on building a sustainable organization to protect what Harold had worked so hard to create. But the executive leaders weren't ready for that—least of all Harold, who denied Steven the oversight of other key people, partly because Harold could see how others perceived Steven's style and personality. In his attempt to protect his daughter, Harold refused to confront Steven and, fearful of antagonizing his father-in-law further, Steven was reluctant to confront Harold. In this case, the best solution for all parties was Steven's decision to exit the family business, as his father-in-law's intractability around granting him a role and responsibility with more authority was so ingrained that a compromise couldn't be reached.

That outcome initially pleased no one and is certainly a danger that families in business together must consider when they fail to recognize personal attributes and don't make expectations and roles clear before a new member comes aboard. Not surprisingly, after Steven obtained a partner's position with the company's public accountant (with Harold's help), family travel resumed.

PAUL'S PERSPECTIVE

My summer experience working with my father included a rotation through different departments and covering for people on vacation, so upon entry, I already had some sense of how each area of the business functioned. When I started full time, as the only family member in my generation, there was an assumption by all, especially me, that I was the heir apparent. This required that I gain more depth of experience in all areas of the business. With only 20 employees, there were no written job descriptions in our business at that time. (I actually wrote them a couple of years later.) My dad would simply give verbal assignments of what he felt needed to be done.

First, there was a responsibility that I was to be first in, last out. I was to be the first one at work in the morning; I had a key to the building, knew the code to the alarm and the combination to the safe, and opened up every day. By the same token, I was usually the last one out of the door because part of my role was assuming stewardship.

Second, I was assigned the task of opening the mail, which may appear menial but was quite revealing. I saw customer orders, checks, and vendor invoices. It gave me a sense of the flow of money in and out of the business. I was also given responsibility for oversight of accounts receivable and the assignment of making collection calls. A small sales territory was assigned, so I knew what it was like to be out on the road with direct customer contact. In addition, I had to be ready to cover in departments if someone was out sick or on vacation.

But my two most important roles and responsibilities involved spending time with my dad. I shadowed him when he met with our accountant, attorney, banker, and insurance and financial advisors, to learn about the inner workings of the business and my father's thought process. The most prized of my duties was having lunch with him every day that I was in the office. I'd pick up sandwiches at the local deli. On Mondays, it was ham and cheese on dark rye—light on the mustard. During our time together, we'd talk a little bit about family and personal stuff, but we'd also talk about business—what was going on, what was working well, what wasn't working well, and what actions we were going to take. I openly sought his guidance and coaching and knew I had to outperform expectations. Though not in writing, my roles and responsibilities were clear and structured from the beginning.

DAVID'S PERSPECTIVE

When I joined my father in the consulting business, I was thirty-nine years old, I'd had many different roles, and I was bringing that combination of experiences to our work together. Still, one of our first conversations concerned exactly who was going to be doing what.

In addition to my role as my dad's partner, consulting with family business clients, one of the things we both felt strongly was that I should run the operations of the business. Since this business was to be the next twenty-five years or more of my life, I should be responsible for everything from payroll to accounts payable, accounts receivable, and invoicing, along with managing the branding, marketing, and sales components of the business. Anything and everything that had to do with the operations of the business was my responsibility. My father certainly had insight into it, and we talked about it all the time, but there was clarity on authority, and the ultimate responsibility to make sure things were getting done was on my shoulders, which made total sense. I truly felt anointed by my dad in the role as president of the company, so I was completely at ease making operational decisions.

But early on, when we were writing an article together, Dad asked me to do a draft of the piece, suggesting that he'd take a look at it, and then we'd post it. So I drafted an article that I thought was pretty good, and I gave it to Dad to review. It came back with red ink all over it, and I instantly had a flashback to high school, when he'd do the same thing to my term papers. Needless to say, it was not a positive feeling. I didn't like it; I'm forty years old, I've done a lot of writing, and I'm a proficient writer, but he's fanatical about the written word. We decided to reverse the roles. Now, we brainstorm an article together, but he writes it, then I edit it, although not nearly as voraciously as he does—and it doesn't trouble him at all. That's an example of looking at one another's best skills and abilities, and it's certainly reduced the chance of any conflict we might otherwise have had.

GUIDELINES FOR SUSTAINABILITY

- Be sure the fit is right before crafting positions for family members—including style and personality in addition to knowledge and skill.

- Don't give favored treatment to children. It doesn't work; there's more at stake than hurt feelings.

- Build a foundation for communication that will enable family members to have open and honest conversations about individual skill sets in the business.

- Have clearly defined roles. We encourage the use of a job description that breaks down the responsibilities of the position into the percentage of time spent on each. (See Addendum #4: Job Description and Time Chart.)

- Obtain clarity in reporting structure, for both individual and corporate accountability.

- Institute regular HR review meetings; there must be candid discussion about who's doing what and what is and is not working.

- Assign roles and responsibilities with an understanding of the individual's attitude, style, personality, and patterns of behavior from years past, so that there isn't the mistake of trapping people into positions that don't play to their strengths.

- Match the strengths of the individual with the needs of the business, and ensure that the principals are aligned on those needs.

- It's not just about *what we do*, it's about *who we are*, and the *who we are* piece is often the guiding factor in determining roles in the business.

- Make sure the senior and younger generation spend lots of time together. That's how the next generation learns.

- Next-gens: seek feedback with an open mind.

- Run a business as a business, not as a family, if your intent is to ensure the health of both for the long run. Families are typically and hopefully based on unconditional love, in accepting each other for who they are. In business, people are accepted and judged based on what they do and how well they do it.

Chapter Four

■ ▦ ■

Decision Making

It's easy to assume that job descriptions and well-defined roles and responsibility guarantee clearly autonomous decision making. But that's not always the case. For a business to be successful, it's critical that there be clarity on the powers of decision making. When we talk about decision making, we're talking about a line of authority because decision making comes with authority, and authority (oftentimes unlike the assignment of a role) is granted once it's earned. In a family business, anyone can buy a pencil sharpener and not need a requisition or permission from others in the company to do so, but when it comes to buying ten acres of land to build a new factory, it's a good idea to run that by senior-level owners and managers in the organization. Somewhere in between the two, guidelines are called for. When the rules and expectations around decision making aren't made clear, the consequences can be significant.

DELEGATING POWERS APPROPRIATELY IS CRITICAL

Decisions are typically most effective when they're made at the most immediate level; we often say that the person who sweeps the floor ought to be the one who decides what kind of a broom to get.

The Stewart family learned this the hard way. This fourth-generation family business was run by an autocratic matriarch who made all the important decisions on her own, despite the fact that her "kids" were in their forties. This was the case for twenty years, so there were no procedures and no policies around how to make decisions, other than asking Mom. She relied largely on her instincts rather than on data to make decisions for this large and capital-intensive enterprise, which required the purchase of multimillion-dollar machines. She didn't look at financial statements; she simply bought what she wanted to, when she wanted to. Her idea of due diligence was just making sure there was enough cash to write the check—literally.

In working with the next generation, it was clear that the future of the business was in jeopardy because of this top-down management style. Despite relative clarity on roles, there was a lack of decision-making ability attached to peoples' jobs, so nobody felt as though they had any authority. Occasionally (almost as a test), Mom would ask the kids to get together with a couple of inept outside advisors (who never knew whose side to take) to make a big decision; they'd meet, argue back and forth, and struggle to a consensus, only to find out that Mom had already made the choice and moved ahead with it. When we questioned why she had done so, she would shrug and say, "They were taking too long." The kids would exit the meeting still arguing, disrupting whatever semblance of harmony existed among their staff.

Part of the delay in the next generation's ability to make a decision was that each of the four kids needed a different level of information to make a decision. This is true of people generally; we all have our individual levels of comfort in terms of how much research or personal experience we need before we're confident enough to make a choice. In this case, those levels were widely divergent, and that's where the dynamic broke down.

Responsibility doesn't guarantee authority. We are currently working to help the Stewarts gain clarity on authority based on their competencies (knowledge, skill, and experience) and the needs of the business to gain Mom's trust and to create clear levels of authority. The desired result: clarity on decision-making responsibility based on the role each plays within the organization and on empowering each to actually have decision-making authority within that area. Second, we're helping them to create a process for decision-making on issues that affect all, starting with a weekly meeting, at which they'll discuss a couple of hot topics, decide what information is required, and then gather that data and move ahead with making the decision.

We're helping to engineer a cultural shift in the decision-making process. Without it, once Mom is out of the picture, sustainability will not be possible. Not surprisingly, Mom is the most difficult family member from whom to get agreement. Her attitude is, "If the kids all agree, *and* I like their decision, I'll go along with it." She's not ready to delegate, and frankly it's doubtful that she ever will be, so the question becomes how her children are going to be able to work with her and, in some instances, even around her, in order to effectively manage the business. At some point, they'll have to put the structure and processes in place today to build a sustainable business without their mother. The Stewart family business is a work in progress.

DECISION MAKING SHOULD BE SHARED, NOT HOARDED

Another client family with issues around decision making is the DeMarcos. Papa DeMarco started the business when he was a young man and has built it into a multimillion-dollar enterprise. He has two sons on board, but despite having given them titles, he simply doesn't allow them to make any important decisions. The problem is similar to the Stewart family's. When you don't truly anoint or empower people so that their decision-making powers are commensurate with their titles, then you're setting up a dynamic of conflict. The older son, Jose, who was named president of the company, has not been empowered to make decisions for two reasons: one, Dad is incredibly controlling, and two, younger brother Juan (CFO) refuses to report to Jose or go along with the rules that Jose lays out. He recognizes that his brother is an empty suit as far as power goes.

This has led to a kind of dysfunction called *triangulation*: when the two brothers can't agree, each complains to Dad about the other, so Dad winds up in the middle of their conflicts. Rather than refusing to engage and insisting they work it out themselves, Dad, who is conflict averse, embraces the role. When they can't agree, he just comes over the top and says, "We're just going to do it this way." He lets younger son Juan get by with no accountability for his actions.

Again, the ultimate consequence in business is losing your job, but so often in family businesses that ultimate consequence doesn't exist, and that's certainly the case with this family. We've repeatedly heard from members of the senior generation, "If he weren't my child, I would fire him." Naturally, this puts the family in an agonizingly difficult situation. With warring dynamics within the family producing a chaotic culture and structure in the business, the end result is conflict, and that's when we get called in. The siblings are constantly fighting; sometimes they don't even know why. In order for them to move forward with appropriate decision-making authority the siblings and their dad must first address the sources of conflict and build agreement to move beyond the past and focus on the future. In this case, that's the partnership between the two brothers and their ability to divide and conquer when it comes to responsibilities and running the business. Once this is achieved, they'll be in a better position to tackle the criteria for making decisions within their respective areas of the business as well as being able to collaborate on "big-picture" decisions involving all.

WHY THESE SENIORS ARE RELUCTANT TO LET GO

Members of the senior generation won't let go until they feel the younger generation is ready to take hold—and that's certainly true in both of these cases. You're not going to let go of the baton if you think the person to whom you're handing it off doesn't have a firm grasp on it. In both examples, the younger generation has not demonstrated the ability to take hold of the business and run it effectively, so there's no way the senior generation is going to let go of absolute control. There's too much at stake. A line we frequently hear from the senior generation is, "I would give my kids much more responsibility and authority if they'd demonstrate competence and just ask for it." And the younger generation says, "I'd love to do so much more and make decisions in this business if Mom or Dad would only let me." Instead of discussing it openly, each waits for the other, and nothing changes, causing a family stalemate.

When power is not granted by the senior generation, it must be taken by the younger generation—although we're not promoting a coup d'état. The younger generation must candidly address obstacles, demonstrate competency, come forward with proposals and well-founded recommendations, and seek the input and approval of the senior generation.

HOW TO CREATE A STRUCTURE THAT SUPPORTS TRANSFER OF DECISION-MAKING POWER

Recently, we worked with the Turner family, owners of a substantial and complex family enterprise with multiple locations. There are five next-gen family members working in the business, all with an ownership stake. Mom and Dad want their children to make decisions, but they don't want them to be able to outvote or rule out one or the other of their siblings. Therefore, we helped them create a formal board of directors and a formal governance structure where all family members sit on the board, along with several outsiders. Major decisions require not only a majority of the family but also a majority of the outside board members. It's an atypical structure, but it's working well and meets the objective Mom and Dad set forth.

We'll talk more about governance in chapter 7, but in our experience a formal structure like this is often quite helpful in guiding the decision-making process. We also introduced the Turners to a "Responsibility Charting" tool. (See Addendum #5: Responsibility Charting.) This brings clarity about who has the responsibility for making decisions, who has the power of veto, who is in a support role (meaning giving advice and recommendations if and when asked for it), and who would be informed.

PAUL'S PERSPECTIVE

Early on, working with my dad, my responsibilities were clear. I was expected to be in the office three days a week and "on the road" in the sales territory two days a week. After about a year of in-depth exposure to all departments, my role inside the office included product pricing and the hiring of new employees, both of which I was trained to do; my dad set forth basic guidelines and granted me decision-making authority. As I developed a deeper understanding of the business and honed my skills in gaining the support of others, I grew into the role of oversight of branch locations and was given further authority to make decisions based on demonstrated ability.

One curious event: just after we made a major acquisition in upstate New York in 1974, which increased our business by about one-third, an abutting territory in Pennsylvania, New Jersey, Delaware, and the balance of New York came open that would more than double our business. The distributor in that marketplace, with nearly identical product lines to ours, was on the verge of bankruptcy. The support of our suppliers would give us an extraordinary opportunity to take over their territory. I wanted to rush in to beat out any competitor and seek the balance of the New York territory. That's when my dad shared a precious story. He told me of the young bull and the old bull standing at the bottom of a hill. The young bull looked up and saw some beautiful cows grazing up the hill and turned to his dad and said, "Pop, look at those beautiful cows, let's run up and service one of them." "No, son," the old bull replied, "let's walk up and service them all." Another lesson learned. We slowed down the process and were ultimately offered the entire territory.

I was executive vice president/COO and vividly remember being in the car with my father when I asked, "Dad, whose decision is this, yours or mine?"

He said, "Whose decision do you think it ought to be?

"I think it ought to be your decision. You're the CEO and principal stockholder."

But he responded, "I think it ought to be your decision."

I sat silent for a few minutes. My wheels were churning. My dad was more of a risk-taker than I, and I also struggled because I was ambivalent. I felt we could handle the balance of the New York territory but knew the acquisition of the entire territory would mean a major change in my life, bringing with it more travel and more time away from my family. Achieving the economies of scale would require a matrix organization, which is more challenging to lead and manage. I also knew the numbers made sense and was energized that it would position us as one of the largest wallcovering distributors in the country. But it was a question of self-confidence at that point in time; I was in my early thirties, without much experience. We'd reviewed the pros and cons, crunched the numbers, and considered the staff. Ultimately, it was my father's expression of confidence in me that gave me the confidence to take the leap of faith; I felt empowered, so we accepted the offer to make the acquisition. In a sense, my father still made that decision because without his support I'd not have done it. The day of the signing, a box of new business cards mysteriously appeared on my desk. They carried the title "President."

Now we were an organization of 250 people with warehouses in four different cities throughout the Northeast, processing close to two thousand transactions a day. I knew I needed a high-functioning team. In the 1970s, Eric Berne and transactional analysis (TA) were in vogue, and I decided I was going to have a TA workshop retreat for our senior-level team. My dad thought I was out of my mind, but I was sold on the idea and hired a professional facilitator.

We looked like nuts; we taped flipcharts on everybody's back, and people went around with magic markers, putting warm fuzzies and cold pricklies on each other's back. It was hysterical but wonderful, and it was the foundation for creating a team. My dad participated eagerly in the process, even though he hadn't liked the idea initially. He trusted me to make that decision.

Shortly after that acquisition, I went through a certificate program called the Owner/President/Managers Program (OMP) at Harvard

Business School, which required ten weeks in residence spread out over a three-year period. When I came back from this program and returned to my office, I immediately saw something was missing: I'd had a brass key on my desk that I used as a paperweight, and it was gone. I knew there was only one person who would have taken that key—my dad. So I went into his office, and asked, "Pop, where's my key?" He assured me that I'd see it again shortly. About three days later, that key appeared, mounted on a piece of green velvet with a glass and walnut frame around it and a plaque underneath that reads, "More important than knowledge is the key to imagination. It can open hearts, minds, doors and even pocketbooks," and it was signed FUF. And I said, "FUF?"

Respectfully imitating Marlon Brando in *The Godfather*, he said, "Frumma U Fatha."

It's magnificent: If my house caught fire, it's among the first things I'd grab. (See Addendum #6: The Key.) His message was, lest I thought I was a "smart ass" with a new piece of parchment, I needed to understand that decisions, the decision-making process, authority, and how you run a business all require imagination as well as knowledge.

One more story. Shortly after I had a private office, people would come to me with questions; sometimes there were two or three people lined up at my door. It was an ego trip. The temptation was to be Solomon-like, handing down judgments, but ultimately I learned that it was more effective for me to question the questioner, asking, "How do you think it ought to be handled? What are the pros and cons? And what do you recommend?" It worked—I empowered others to make decisions and to feel comfortable with them, and the business ran smoothly—but I have to admit, it was lonely without that line of people at my door!

DAVID'S PERSPECTIVE

When I first came into the business with my father, we established a clear understanding of our respective roles and the decisions each would make. Operationally, I was coming in as the president of the company, and my responsibilities included consulting with business families and business development, as well as everything involved in business operations. Dad was comfortable with my making those decisions because ultimately I was the one who had to own them and be accountable, whether it was choosing marketing tools, converting to QuickBooks, revamping our website, switching CRM tools, and hiring an assistant, to participating in events and conferences, and even writing this book.

One of the things we put into practice early on was a dollar limit on decisions; on anything that cost under $1,000, either one of us had the ability to make a decision without consulting with the other. Anything above that figure we agreed to discuss first, even though the final decision would be mine.

While we reserve the right to have differing opinions regarding client matters and often express them in front of our clients, we deliberately model how to disagree and not be disagreeable. When we have disagreements regarding other business matters, we welcome each other's opinion and work them out in private, with clear knowledge of where the decision-making authority lies. Putting in practice what we teach, our support of one another in front of others is unequivocal. Open communication is a big piece of what makes us successful.

When I was rebranding our website, we both felt that it needed a facelift. My father had an emotional attachment to the company logo; it had the company name, Transition Consulting Group (see Addendum #7: Old TCG Logo), and was a relatively large logo that required a lot of vertical real estate on a webpage, so everything else on the opening page would drop below the fold, meaning you couldn't see anything else when you first open the site. The logo had to be reworked, and Dad had a hard time initially accepting that necessity. Even though it was my decision to make as part of operations, we had a respectful, sensitive discussion about it. It wasn't a question of me just grabbing the authority and running with it; I wanted my father's understanding and agreement.

Respect runs in two directions; I was bringing a lot of change into a business that Dad had been running for twenty years, and he had his own ways of doing things: his handwritten Day-Timer calendar, a three-by-five index card billing system, etc. For a single-person enterprise, his systems worked just fine—but with a partner added to the mix, we had to create an environment in which we could both see what was happening. I set up a simple but efficient spreadsheet that allows us to track our clients and is accessible to both of us. It allows me to do the billing efficiently because all I have to do is open up the spreadsheet. We use shared electronic calendars now, too. Switching from paper to digital isn't easy to do, but Dad was unbelievably open to these changes, in part, I think, because he knew they needed to happen, and in part because of the way in which I presented them to him—again, with respect for his expertise and history with the business and with open discussion. I also think that since I had worked outside the family business for several years and was bringing many of the skills and experiences I had gained during that time away, my father trusted the decisions I was making because I had gone through this process before.

If the younger generation just comes in and bulldozes through things without understanding the culture of the business, then they're not going to have the level of success they would have had they just moved methodically through the process.

GUIDELINES FOR SUSTAINABILITY

- Earn decision-making authority; earn the trust.

- Make decisions based on those most affected by them.

- Don't base decisions on instinct alone. Trust your gut, but get good data.

- When there are disagreements, battle it out in the boardroom—but when you walk out of that room, everyone must be in support of one another. This is critical because otherwise the rest of your staff will see that you're not aligned, creating chaos and infighting as they try to decide with whom they should ally.

- Be sure that whoever is empowered has the knowledge, skill, and experience commensurate with the responsibility.

- Gain agreement and clarity on "who has decision-making authority over what."

- Set clear boundaries and limits of authority on decision making.

- When the next generation enters, prepare for change and get ready to embrace it.

- In order for a new generation to run with the baton, the previous generation must let go.

- Recognize that seniors won't let go until they see the next generation ready to take hold.

- Be willing to take risks—and it's all right for the senior generation to let the younger generation make some mistakes.

- Give the next generation enough room in the business to make mistakes and learn from them.

- Acquire self-confidence; it is a prerequisite to effective decision making.

- Be willing to empower others.

- Establish a process that ensures follow-through and accountability.

- Build on the ideas of others. It validates them and gives you an ally in a joint effort.

- Next-gens: be sensitive to the senior generation's possible resistance to change, and openly discuss it so you can build alignment together.

Chapter Five

■ ■ ■

Family Gatherings: The Foundations for Stewardship

You may be familiar with the family watchmaking business, Patek Philippe; their tagline is, "You never actually own a Patek Philippe. You merely look after it for the next generation." That sense of preservation and passing along what matters is key to the continued success of a family business.

IT IS CRUCIAL FOR A FAMILY BUSINESS TO ESTABLISH A FIRM FOUNDATION FOR STEWARDSHIP

The extent to which family members are aligned and united in their understanding of their shared culture, history, and values sets the foundation for the enterprise. It's a responsibility that family members and businesses have to one another, to their legacy, to future generations, and to the business itself and all the families it supports.

There's a great saying: "The family that plays together, stays together," and we believe that family members spending time together help create those integral intergenerational bonds and encourage the right type of communication. A structure for family meetings and communication fosters stewardship. It allows the upcoming generation to learn about the history of the business, the highs and lows, and what it took for previous generations to bring the business to where it is today. Good communication lets us share not just the great events but also the more difficult issues the business has faced or is facing. When family meetings or gatherings are part of the culture of the family early on, the younger members grow up knowing they have a forum in which to address everything with respect to the family enterprise.

Family meetings are more important as the family expands. Siblings who grow up in the same household hopefully learn to appreciate, respect, and trust one another, but often the relationship between cousins is not so close. As the nuclear family expands and children get married and create their own families, core values become merged with those of their spouses, creating new and sometimes differing value systems. Spending more time with adult siblings and cousins creates a greater level of understanding, trust, and respect for differences in style and personality.

One of our favorite quotes is from our friend Fredda Herz Brown in her book *Reweaving the Family Tapestry*: "Stories are the fabric from which the family is woven." Family gatherings are the forum, and family stories set the stage and are the foundation upon which both the family and the business are built.

HOW TO CREATE OPPORTUNITIES TO BOND

For some, the opportunity to bond may involve regular family get-togethers; for others, it could be a family-only website for sharing news, family reunions, and travel. Some create a video or write a book that chronicles the family and business history, as did the Zildjian family (the oldest business of record in the United States) with *Zildjian: A History of the Legendary Cymbal Makers* or Mitzi

Perdue's book about her late husband, *Tough Man, Tender Chicken: Business and Life Lessons from Frank Perdue.*

HOW TO DEFINE "FAMILY"

Years ago, we met with a family discussing the future of corporate stock ownership. One sibling said, "It should go to bloodline direct descendants of Grandpa." Another said, "What about spouses? They're family members, too." Then a third chimed in: "Well, let's draw the line at adopted children. They're not Grandpa's bloodline, but they're still family." And a fourth said, "Wait just a minute, the children from my common-law husband's first marriage are as much family to me as any of you are!" What started as a simple question rapidly turned into a conflict as four siblings tried to come up with an acceptable definition of the word "family." Of course, this isn't unique; modern families are often blended, extended, and even mended, making the definition of lines rather complex. We actually worked with one family where two people who worked together didn't realize they were cousins until they saw each other at a family meeting.

As an example of how to create an enduring family structure, consider the Zildjian family, the largest manufacturer of cymbals in the world, whose business was established in Constantinople in 1623. We held a family meeting with Armand Zildjian, his wife, his children, and his grandchildren. The then-fifteenth-generation teenagers and preteens sat in rapt attention as Papa Armand shared stories and talked about the history of the business. As the values behind his stories emerged, we wrote them on a flip chart and then had the preteens create a family crest that was an expression of those values. The family brought us in for this event because they wanted to make sure that Grandfather's values were, in fact, passed on. It was a precious and significant experience for everyone.

Another family, the Thompsons, asked us to facilitate a family meeting with three generations of family members. They have a large family business, attached to substantial real estate: a family ranch compound with thousands of acres. Their great-grandfather and his siblings who started the business had created this compound with the idea of keeping the family together; family members could not have ownership in one without the other, and the legal structure precluded any disentanglement, which prevented a family member who did not wish to have equity in the business from having an interest in the compound. The founders hadn't foreseen the potential consequences of their actions, despite their good intentions. Their wish was to create an environment in which the family was together: together at work, together in play. But the result actually constrained the family because some of them didn't want to be part of one but wanted to be part of the other, whether it was the business or the compound.

With leadership of the operating companies well under control, the senior generation was looking to pass along the management of this property to the younger folks, and it was a massive responsibility. We facilitated a one-and-a-half-day retreat at the family estate and did breakouts by generation, helping each to understand the values and needs of the other and clarifying the roles each would play in managing the property.

We gathered all the family members in a giant circle, and then had them write out all the different responsibilities that were involved in maintaining the property and designate a lead person for each. The younger generation stretched from the midthirties down into the teens, and what emerged was a real sense of autonomy by the younger generation to start to take hold and make decisions. They created committees: a social committee to run the calendar, a landscape committee, a house committee to see to maintenance, a boat committee, etc. Despite not coming to a resolution to the dismantling of the property from the business (the lawyers are working on that now), the Thompson family retreat accomplished the aims that their ancestors hoped to see—the next-gen coalescing, stepping up, and taking ownership of their legacy and inheritance.

Contrast the Thompson happy outcome with that of another family that never held family meetings. In this case, the grandfather had purchased a beautiful oceanfront property and bequeathed it to his three grandchildren, three close siblings. But when their grandfather died, one of them wanted to sell the property, one wanted to fix it up and rent it out, and the third wanted to buy it outright from her sibs but lacked the means to do so. Now these three previously close siblings were at odds with each other, the furthest thing from their grandfather's intent. Had there been family discussions around Grandfather's objectives and their potential consequences prior to his death, this might have been avoided.

Another family was at odds after the death of the patriarch and founder, Max. Family members openly spoke harshly about one another in a way that would certainly have undercut public perception of their high-profile name. We helped Max's three children and their spouses (in their sixties) and his adult grandchildren establish family meetings to effectively force the family to come together. There was a massive estate to deal with, and because they were all joint heirs, they needed to come to some meeting of the minds about how to deal with it—but Max had been the glue that held the family together, and now they were splintered into factions. We began talking about Max's values—those they wished to preserve, abandon, and add. After creating a code of conduct (see Addendum #8: Max's Family Code of Conduct), we helped the family convert the values into concrete goals and convert the goals into action steps on which the family could align and work toward some common ends. We helped them to gain listening skills and to speak in a manner in which they could be heard. This was especially challenging because they were in the habit of talking over each other. They will be tasked with making decisions about the estate for years to come, and now with an effective way to communicate and quarterly family meetings, they will be more adept at meeting the challenges and opportunities that lie ahead.

PAUL'S PERSPECTIVE

I vividly recall the Friday night dinners at my father's parents' home with his two brothers and wives and my cousins, a total of fifteen people. My cousins and I still have the supportive and loving relationships that were nurtured through those family gatherings. I recall how my cousins and I would sit on the floor of my grandmother's den, laughing hysterically as Uncle Herman, my grandmother's brother from New York, was holding court. A tall, imposing man, he would share ribald stories. My grandmother could overhear him from the other room and would yell, "Shtilh, Herman, the kinder!" But Uncle Herman would just keep going.

We had wonderful times together; when we couldn't find a football to toss around in the backyard, we'd swipe a loaf of pumpernickel bread from Nana's freezer. And there was the time when one cousin dangled my brother out of the attic window by his feet, just as my grandmother drove up to the house. Even today, we recall these stories, and as light as they are, the humor and deep sense of camaraderie still tightens the bond that keeps our family together. This was especially important for my uncles and their sons, who enjoyed a long and successful run together in their family business. Eventually, many of us will end up in a family cemetery that has plots for four generations—another way in which we're joined.

At family gatherings with my mom's family, my grandmother would share stories of how she and my grandfather immigrated to the United States as young teenagers, how she learned to speak perfect English with no trace of a European accent, how my grandfather smuggled his hearing- and speech-impaired brother to the United States in a trunk, and the challenges they faced starting their own business. Their extraordinary courage, care for family, willingness to take risks, and perseverance—all remarkable, all indelible in the culture of our business family, all values I hope will endure for generations yet to come.

In raising our daughter and son, my wife and I believed in transparency and made it part of our family culture and values. When my wife and I planned a trip to Africa, David said to me, "Dad, you need to tell me what's going on. What if a lion eats you?" So I sat down with him, opened my spreadsheet, and showed him a detailed balance sheet and where everything was. He said, "Dad, we need to talk." I said, "We just did." He said, "No. You showed me some numbers. We need to *talk*."

David said, "What if the lion doesn't just swallow you but just spits you out? What do you and Mom want in terms of long-term care? Do you want to be in a nursing home? Do you want to be at home? Do you want heroic measures to keep you alive?" As the conversation continued, we talked about a continuing care community, wills, trusts, trustees, and so forth. We even got into what kind of caskets we wanted. We update this conversation periodically with our children and financial advisors and even morphed it into a published article, "The Dress Rehearsal," that appears on our website.

DAVID'S PERSPECTIVE

When I was growing up, we always took family trips, and it was a great way to be able to disconnect from our busy worlds and be together as a family. We went to Puerto Rico a couple of times; we took trips to Mexico and the Caribbean; Dad took a sabbatical from work, and we took a summer off and went to France for six weeks. Those memories are wonderful and helped to build the healthy family dynamic we have today.

We take a lot of trips with our own kids now, sometimes with my in-laws. Almost every year we visit different places together, and it provides us with the opportunity to share time and experiences beyond our usual daily lives and to see the world as a family. We took a trip to Israel two years ago, which was an unbelievable journey and a wonderful learning experience to have with my family. I'm pleased my father and mother made travel a family tradition, one we can now share with our own children.

Family dinners are also an important part of our lives, as they were growing up in my family of origin. When my son was young, he introduced us to the concept of "recognizing" each other at the table. This became part of our routine; first, we go around the table, and each person expresses appreciation and recognizes others for something they've done. We then end by sharing our favorite part of the day. It's a way to elicit meaningful conversation, reflection, and gratitude on all of our parts, to step outside of the daily buzz of activity to acknowledge how important each family member is to the whole group. Wonderful, wide-ranging conversations ensue at the table about history, politics, sports—everything and anything.

Everyone has a chance to contribute, to be heard, and to hear each other's opinions. These are our mini-family meetings, and they contribute to the family culture of the larger family meetings the kids will participate in down the line. My son's "recognition" tradition has grown into a family-wide happening; when we get together with our extended families, we also take the time to recognize and thank one another, to share and appreciate each other's contributions. It's a deeply warm and touching experience, and I think everyone gets a lot out of it.

Each year, our family, the ten of us (my parents, my sister and brother-in-law, their daughter and son, my wife and our son and daughter, plus an occasional dog or two), go to my parents' home on Cape Cod for July 4th weekend and again over Labor Day, which is around my children's and father's birthdays. We use that as an opportunity to celebrate, be together as a family, and engage in discussions beyond the daily grind.

My wife and I recently updated our wills, as they had not been touched since our children were born. When it came time to discuss guardianship in the event something happens to my wife and me, we felt it was important to include our children in this conversation. Although it was a difficult topic to discuss, our children were at the ages (seventeen and thirteen) where they deserved to have a voice in the discussion. They both appreciated being part of the process, as difficult as the conversation was for them.

Philanthropy has always been an important part of our family culture. My parents have instilled the value of philanthropy in us since we were young, and would make matching contributions to whatever charities we chose so that our gifts would go further. My wife and I have carried that over with our children. It helps promote giving back, which is so important. As we did as kids, our children work together to choose a charity they agree is the most deserving, which encourages good communication and coming to a consensus.

The year of the Boston Marathon bombing, my father and mother sat down with our kids and told them how they'd given financial gifts to two brothers who'd each lost a leg in the bombing, so each of them could enjoy a special experience after they'd recovered.

After they told the story, my then ten-year-old daughter left the table, went upstairs, returned with a crisp five-dollar bill, handed it to my dad, and said, "Papa, please give this to them for me."

This year, my daughter Lily had her Bat Mitzvah, and instead of having a traditional service, she wanted to take that time to get everybody together to make a contribution to a charity called Cradles to Crayons, an organization that collects clothing and other supplies for children in need. There is a facility at which volunteers work sorting items and creating packages for the kids. My daughter ran a month-long clothing drive that literally filled our two-car garage with donations, and on the day of her Bat Mitzvah we held an event in our backyard with more than seventy family and friends who came and sorted through the clothing. The charity sent a representative, and it was an amazing afternoon that generated packages for over 550 kids.

Clearly, the family tradition of philanthropy is alive and well in the next generation.

GUIDELINES FOR SUSTAINABILITY

- Instill a sense of stewardship in the next generation early on.

- Spend time with family members to create better respect for differences.

- Chronicle the family and business history; consider a book or a video.

- Share stories and distill the values that emerge.

- Allow everyone a voice.

- Strengthen the bonds of affection and loyalty.

- Engage and empower the younger generation in making decisions together.

- Use family meetings as a forum for open dialogue to address challenges and disagreements.

- Align on goals.

- Acknowledge the value of the family name.

- Create a code of conduct.

- Play together, laugh together, plan together, contribute together.

- Have a "dress rehearsal" to talk about end-of-life issues and desires. It is easier when initiated by the older generation, so don't wait for the kids to bring it up.

- Make sure your will is in order and up to date. We are always amazed at how many otherwise savvy people neglect essential estate-planning basics. We've actually worked with funeral directors who didn't have wills; talk about denial!

- Involve the younger generation in philanthropic decisions.

Chapter Six

■ ▨ ■

Strategic Planning

HOW WILL YOU KNOW WHAT'S REQUIRED OF THE NEXT GENERATION OF LEADERS?

Strategic planning has long been correlated with the survival of family businesses. Like so many processes in family enterprise, it comes in all shapes and sizes. Given the massive pace of change—economic, technological, and social—coupled with the diverse interests of family members, we suggest that strategic plans be cast in Jell-O rather than in cement. While the basics of strategic planning include an understanding of the business's history; a clear definition of its mission and purpose; and an understanding of its marketplace and its strengths, limitations, threats, and opportunities, we encourage family business members to craft a process that meets their unique requirements. It's more than monitoring and reacting to a dashboard of key performance indicators.

COOKIE-CUTTER SOLUTIONS DON'T WORK

We're neither suggesting nor designing a specific process. Rather, our goal in this chapter is to suggest the compelling need to engage in a strategic planning process. The biggest difference between planning in a family enterprise is, of course, the family: its culture and history, its values and character, the needs and desires of multiple individuals, and how each of those intersects with the business itself. As a family moves from one generation to the next, this becomes more complex as more and more variables must be considered—more participants in the process and differing generational styles, perspectives, and desires. Plus, there's an age-old question: "Does the family serve the business, or does the business serve the family?" and the answer can vary from generation to generation and even from year to year. For example, if illness suddenly strikes a key family member who has a major stake in the business, how will that impact the strategy of the business? And how will the strategy of the business impact the family? Or a family business could be just plodding along when an offer from a competitor comes along that quickly changes the course of business.

STRATEGIC PLANNING CAN BE A TOOL FOR TEAM BUILDING AND ALIGNMENT

For some, strategic planning may mean continuing to build on the founder's vision. For others, it may mean a process that allows for enormous change. For some, the process may include participation by just the owners. For others, it might include only those owners working in the business. A typical process includes senior management, which may be a blend of family members and nonfamily members, especially those who will have the responsibility for the implementation of the plan. There is no right or wrong; it all depends on the family and the business situation *at that moment in time* and must be revisited on a routine basis.

Most importantly, the team walks out of a well-conducted strategic planning session with a much clearer vision and alignment as to where they want to take their organization. It's impossible to move smoothly when you have people pulling in many different directions. After a properly run strategic planning session, suddenly everyone's on the bus, in the right seats, and moving in the same direction together.

THE BEST-LAID PLANS . . .

A good example of how strategic planning has the potential to create alignment is the Greenberg family, a fourth-generation family business with several hundred people run by three cousins. The vision for the business wasn't consistent among the senior team or the family members. They had an elaborate dashboard that monitored key indicators in the business, but they only focused on the numbers within each of their respective silos, and they weren't focusing on strategy. Each of the cousins held his or her own narrow vision of the whole; they needed to come together to gain a broader perspective.

They hired a family friend to engage in a strategic planning process consisting of multiple full-day, off-site meetings with upward of fifteen of the senior team leaders. Their planning sessions were held for two days a month over three months, utilizing different exercises, and culminating in a plan that would be executed by the team. The process appeared to go well, and some exciting strategies emerged. Unfortunately, however, it's not all about the process: if the plan is not subsequently executed on that process, then both process and plan become irrelevant—and this organization simply did not execute on the plan that they'd supposedly agreed upon.

The reason in this case was the dysfunction level of the family. Superficially, the cousins seemed aligned and eager to succeed—but beneath the surface, there was disagreement about what the individual family members wanted out of the business and what they wanted to do with this business, which led to a tremendous internecine power struggle. Though they participated actively in the planning stages, they were severely conflict averse and they withheld their disagreements. When it came time for implementation, the issues beneath the surface began to bubble up. That's when we were called in.

A big contributor to their problems was the cousins' almost exclusive attention to the areas in which they felt safest—their myopic laser focus on individual silos. There was one family member in sales, one in operations, and one in finance. There's often natural conflict in businesses between sales, operations, and finance—but as we all know, it's how the conflict is managed that makes the difference. What each of them wanted to do in his or her silo was so individual it prevented them from having the perspective from what we call "The Horizontal Bar" (see Addendum #9: The Horizontal Bar), which looks across the entire organization. With the absence of routine ownership meetings and "big-picture" discussions, they couldn't differentiate between the best interests of the entire organization versus the best interests of a particular department.

What had started as a strategic planning process turned into intense consulting to help the cousins understand and unravel the underlying issues that prevented them from achieving alignment. The strategic plan was an unfortunate casualty of their dysfunctional communication and "me first" thinking, and the culprit was the failure of their facilitator to first ensure they could be candid and able to manage disagreements.

A different scenario is presented by a second-generation family business run by the Swan family. Many management gurus suggest business owners need to spend at least 20 percent of their time thinking strategically about their businesses, but often, as with this family, owners are too caught up in the day-to-day running of the business to take that three-thousand-foot view.

With a long history of successes behind them, the Swan family's business became one of the leaders in its field. Family members were spending all their time working *in* the business, not *on* the business, when what they needed to do was step back, take a deep breath, and consider the long game plan. We began our work with the family to ensure they had the foundation of effective communication: the willingness to be candid and the ability to disagree and not be disagreeable. Together, we performed a simplistic SLOT Analysis and explored organizational strengths and limitations and the opportunities and threats the organization might have to manage. Strengths and limitations focus on the internal components of the business: the opportunities and threats focus on the external components of the business, the market, the industry, competitors, new opportunities, etc.

Strengths (Internal)	Limitations (Internal)
Opportunities (External)	Threats (External)

Team building was a big component of this process; we worked with the six senior team members, four of whom were family members, to develop specific actions that would capitalize on their strengths and opportunities and minimize the risks presented by their limitations and threats.

They were also able to share their thoughts about their own personal strengths and limitations and how well they were in sync with the needs of the company, including the opportunities they wished to pursue and the threats in need of management. Ultimately, they agreed on a new direction for the business, rebuilt their staffing, and rebranded, down to a complete redesign of their website and logo. The process played out over a couple of months in four half-day meetings. One of the most gratifying results was that two family members who'd been at odds when the process began shared a big hug at its end, acknowledging this process had helped pull them together.

We've been working with this organization on and off over a year and a half, and we just got a call from the CEO saying he wants to go through the process again, to rethink the plan based on the changes in the organization since the original plan was created. They constantly revisit their plan to measure where they are in terms of their success and planned growth, and now that they're nearing the accomplishment of the specific goals that they'd wanted to achieve, they know it's time to return to the planning process and do it again.

THERE'S ALSO A PERSONAL APPLICATION

Just as you look at a SLOT analysis to assess strengths, limitations, opportunities, and threats of the business, sometimes it's important to do the equivalent with key family members, looking at their likes, dislikes, strengths, and limitations. It's ideal for people to function in the areas of their greatest strengths—their "unique brilliance"—rather than the areas of their limitations. Abundant research shows that the investment in reinforcing strengths pays far greater dividends than does bolstering limitations. As family members perform this exercise individually and open themselves to feedback from others, it leads to insights for the individual and also promotes candid dialogue, new appreciation for one another's worth, and opportunities for enhanced planning when family members start thinking in the same direction.

STRATEGIC PLANNING IS NOT A ONE-TIME EVENT

It's a dynamic, ongoing process, and it must be rethought and revamped as the company changes. The process will vary depending on the needs of the family and the business at any moment in time. Part of it is contingency planning, asking, "What if this happened? What if that happened? How would we handle it?" A good plan is more than a road map; it's an atlas.

PAUL'S PERSPECTIVE

In the mid-1980s, the wallcovering industry started to peak. As consumption declined, manufacturers produced more patterns in an attempt to maintain market share. This required a higher investment in inventory for distributors such as us. More inventory in a declining market resulted in less turnover, and the frequency of inventory turns is critical for a distributor's success. Add tighter margins due to more competitive pricing and we were set up for the perfect storm.

Meanwhile, another factor was at play. While I saw value in our business and at times truly enjoyed what I was doing, a part of my soul wanted to head in another direction. I knew something had to change and hired a strategic planning facilitator from Chicago with whom I had worked for our trade association. Together with senior managers, we drilled through the basics.

Over the course of a couple of days, it became clear that it was essential for us to control our own destiny. The strategic options that surfaced were the expansion of our retail business, converting (performing all the functions of a manufacturer except the actual printing), or partnering with/acquiring a manufacturing facility. We had tried to buy a couple of manufacturing facilities a few years earlier, but we were unable to put together a deal. The more I reflected on our options, the more I realized I did not have sufficient confidence in the industry to invest further capital and put our business and the more than 250 families it supported at risk. This strategic planning process ultimately led me, as the sole owner at that point, to make a decision that was hibernating at a preconscious level—to sell the business.

DAVID'S PERSPECTIVE

Full disclosure: Even planners must make time for strategic planning. Being humans ourselves, we, too, got caught up in running the day-to-day business and lost sight of our long-term game plan. For the last several years, we've enjoyed steady growth, especially with the creation of The Peer Alliance (peer groups for family businesses). My father and I wanted to keep this business between the two of us for a while, to enjoy being a team working with our clients and facilitating family business peer groups. And we were very much in an execution mode for the last three years—but we ultimately hit a point where it was tough to get to that next echelon of growth because we were close to capacity in our ability to manage clients and peer groups. That's a good thing, of course, but if we wanted to jump to that next level, we had to step back and be a bit more strategic.

For me, as CEO, I needed to think seriously about what I wanted for the next twenty years. For my father, it was about what he wanted for the next five or so years. It required a new mind-set for me; I needed to learn how to leverage our company beyond just the two of us if I wanted to grow it beyond what my father and I were already doing. I talked with my dad about what I wanted long term from the business, to hear what he was thinking, and to create a plan that would get us both where we wanted to be.

What I realized was that even we, who do this for others, could not effectively lead ourselves in the process, that we too needed the assistance of a facilitator because it's too challenging to be both a participant and a facilitator. Realizing that, I engaged with a business coach whose focus was training entrepreneurs to leverage themselves and their businesses for growth. Through a series of modules, on-site training, and a community of entrepreneurs, I learned better how to position our company for growth and sustainability. In addition to significant changes in our marketing approach, the simple addition of a virtual assistant to the team has enabled us to let go of some of the day-to-day tasks that were critical yet didn't drive our business forward. We have now freed ourselves to focus on more strategic areas, positioning us for growth.

I was challenged to step out of my comfort zone and look at what wasn't right in front of my face—and that's the beauty of the strategic planning process. It encourages people to think differently and to think beyond what might just be in front of them. It lets you consider the "if," which may in fact be something you have some control over and hadn't previously thought about. It pushed me to use skills I had but which were perhaps underutilized.

One byproduct of our strategic planning process is this book, along with rebranding, new marketing, and, of course, a concrete plan that we're going to execute against (and I know I'm accountable for that), one that leads us to growth within the company, allowing us to serve even more families.

GUIDELINES FOR SUSTAINABILITY

- Create a dashboard to measure and chart key performance indicators, but don't let that be the only factor that drives your business.

- Set aside time to think strategically, but cast the plans in Jell-O, not cement.

- Resist a "one-size-fits-all" process; design a process that meets your needs at this moment in time. Be sure the principals are prepared to address sensitive issues with candor and skill.

- Be sure the key players are ultimately aligned and support the plan.

- Execute on the plan; assure accountability for implementation.

- Have a process for feedback and evaluation. Review it frequently.

- Start planning again when you're close to achieving your goals.

- Hire a facilitator so you can be an effective participant.

- Use a wide-angle lens; explore unthinkable options.

- Recognize there are times for the business to serve the family.

- Realize that sometimes strategic planning can lead to unexpected results.

- Find your unique brilliance and exploit it for your own benefit and that of the business.

Chapter Seven

■ ■ ■

Governance Structures

As we can attest, it's lonely at the top for the CEO of a family business. Unlike leaders in nonfamily enterprises, you can't necessarily go home and unload to your spouse about the challenges you have with your colleagues at the office, because it's family, and it can get sticky. Two sibling partners in business together can have an argument, the language can get foul, the insults can get strong—yet the next morning everyone forgets about it, and they'll greet each other with a hug. But if one goes home at the end of the day and proceeds to tell his spouse that he just had an argument with his brother and it got nasty, the brother will forget, but the spouse may never forget, and there's a risk of creating an inappropriate level of hostility. It's a good idea to have others to whom you can vent.

This no doubt contributes to the statistical data that shows family businesses with boards have a higher survival rate. An effective governance structure is one of the most important tools for sustainability. Governance comes in multiple forms. While a board of directors is a legal entity charged with representing the interests of all shareholders for the governance of the business and the oversight of the CEO, advisory boards, which are popular among smaller family businesses, are not legal entities. Rather, they serve at the will of the CEO and function in a strictly advisory, non-legally-binding capacity. Their focus is typically at the strategic level. Both boards function at the intersection of the family, the ownership, and the management of the business. (See Addendum #10: Multi-Roles Model.)

BOARD OF DIRECTORS OR ADVISORY BOARD

In many family enterprises, boards of directors perform a perfunctory function of no real value, but increasingly, enterprising families are creating legal structures to support the interests of all stakeholders. Unlike an advisory board, the role of a board of directors is specific, guided by jurisdiction and corporate bylaws. (See Addendum #11: Common Role of Family Business Board of Directors.) Whether a board of directors or an advisory board, member roles must be clear to avoid confusion and even chaos—as in the case of a daughter, newly appointed to the board, who decided to change the artwork in the executive offices and the contents of the cafeteria vending machines.

Boards provide structure, discipline, focus, and accountability. But here's a note of caution: if you're not ready to listen to the opinions and advice of others, then don't create a board, and if you're not willing to plan and invest energy in preparation and follow-through, then don't waste your time and that of others.

While board members seldom serve strictly for financial reasons, we often recommend compensation of board members at least equal to that of the CEO on his or her per diem basis. Why? Because it's important that the family, including the CEO, sees the board members having comparable value.

The Dean family had a nonfamily/nonshareholder president who had been running the business for thirty years, hired by the client's father. None of the six children (in their sixties) worked in the business or were willing and able to run the company; all had other careers: one doctor, two teachers, an artist, and two dilettantes.

There were four nonfamily board members with a mean age of seventy-five. This had been the father's board, and there were no term limits; some members had been there for twenty years. There was no process for CEO succession or for the evaluation of the effectiveness of the board. At the meeting we attended, one board member fell asleep! Three family members sat on the board but weren't involved in any way in the business; they were there primarily to ensure they got additional distributions to support already-extravagant lifestyles.

This ineffective board functioned as parents to the kids asking for bigger allowances. Meetings were fraught with bickering and discontent. It felt as though we were at a kitchen table with an all-too-familiar dysfunctional family rather than at a business meeting.

In a meeting with the shareholders, we shared our observations. We recommended that they consider some changes, including the retirement of two elders on the board. The siblings were reluctant to make these changes. The chair of the board, who was one of the teachers, was conflict averse. She didn't know how to manage her siblings and was uneasy about disturbing what little harmony remained in the family.

These siblings were poor communicators and constantly at odds, unable to run a structure that was in the best interests of the business. The company president took advantage of that to run it as he saw fit, without the advice of anyone. The real challenge in this case was that the president wanted to reinvest in and grow the company in the best interests of his bonus plan and was getting fed up with excessive distributions. Without an effective board and without this president, the company would have been in real trouble.

We recommended that the siblings retain an industry expert to help preserve the golden goose and look at the needs of the business over the next five to ten years and restructure their board, adding term limits and bringing on members who could help drive the vision of the business.

We recommended, too, that they begin a search for their next CEO and use the new board as a tool to do this. The business employed close to four hundred people, so there were four hundred families affected, not just the family that owned it. There was a lot on the line.

Here's a client story where the board saved the business. Pam and Julie are twins. They're equally skilled, equally educated, and equally experienced in their parents' rapidly expanding chain of retail stores. Mom and Dad created a board of advisors to support the twins in later years and to serve as a tie-breaking body in the unlikely event of conflict between their children. The board also helped to guide the strategic direction of the business, including several acquisitions, geographic expansion, and diversification.

The board of advisors was in place for five years and required extensive preparation, a task that fell on the twins. While the board provided value, the twins did not see it worthy of their investment of time and energy and thus urged it be disbanded. One year later, the twins, in their thirties, faced an unexpected tragedy when their father died at age fifty-four. There was no contingency plan, and Mom was emotionally unstable and unable to participate in the business.

We were hired to help recreate a board of advisors to guide the twins and provide the business with a sustainable plan. We had extensive discussions about the goals of the twins to ensure their alignment; we also talked with key executives and learned about the business, helped set criteria the advisors had to meet, and then facilitated a search for candidates with skill sets in areas that matched the critical success factors of the business and the personalities and styles compatible with the family and the enterprise. We helped the twins conduct interviews, make appointment decisions, orient the new advisors, and create a process for evaluation. Their new board is working well, and gives the twins the support they need as they transition to new leadership roles.

ENSURE APPROPRIATE BOARD MEMBERSHIP

Cain Ventures is an old-line conservative southern enterprise with holdings in multiple businesses. Their board has been effective in its governance role, providing a structure and a process for decision making while serving the interests of a diverse set of family members. We were hired to facilitate the creation of entry guidelines for the next generation, G4. When the company's chairman and CEO introduced us at a board meeting, he went around the room with introductions, person by person, "This is my brother Chad, my second cousin Gwen, my Aunt Susan," and so on until he abruptly paused, with glaring daggers at the guy across the table, and said, "and *this* is a new board member, my ex-wife's second husband, Frank."

Frank had a grin from ear to ear as a distinct chill overpowered the room. Clearly, the chairman's wife held enough stock to put her second husband on the board. Our subsequent work with the family obviously not only addressed entry policies and rules of engagement but also Frank's presence and his impact on a heretofore harmonic and aligned board and the advisability of tighter restrictions on stock ownership. In addition to an ex-spouse's second mate, we typically discourage board membership of the company attorney, accountant, banker, retired employees, personal friends, and sometimes even the family business consultant. For the most part, their perspectives are already known, and board seats should be held by those with knowledge and experience matching the critical success factors of the business. Board members need to be selected not simply for their industry knowledge and experience. Personality and style also count. Effective boards communicate well and comfortably. They are communities of trust, respect, and candor.

THE ROLE OF THE FAMILY COUNCIL

The need for governance, of course, applies not only to the business but to the family as well, and increasingly we see families creating family councils—structures that evolve from family meetings.

The role of the family council differs significantly from the role of the board of directors. They're typically a small group with multiple generations and different family branches functioning as decision-making bodies, representing the interests of family members both with regard to the business and other matters as well. Some family councils organize family vacations, others address educational funding, and still others make decisions on family investments and philanthropy. The ultimate goal of family councils is to provide a forum in which family members can communicate effectively, build and maintain relationships with one another, and preserve the culture and the values of the family.

Family councils can also provide great opportunities for leadership experience for rising generations; when younger members of the family are empowered to be part of the decision-making process, whether it's about a family vacation or a family website or projects and gifts to other family members, it gives them a voice, and this is perhaps its greatest benefit. Everyone on a family council gains by hearing others and being heard. The Thompson family in chapter 5 is a wonderful model of this.

We encourage current and emerging leaders to participate actively on other boards, whether philanthropic or business related. By participating on other boards, they learn how a board functions, what works well and what doesn't, when and why it's important to provide input, and how to build on the contributions of others. Recognizing this need was a driving factor in our creation of The Peer Alliance, to give younger leaders their own advisory board.

PAUL'S PERSPECTIVE

When I was a youngster, on Thursday nights we typically went out for dinner to the local Chinese restaurant. About once a month, Dad would turn to my brother, our mother, and me and say, "Okay. On the count of three," and we knew what that meant. We all said, "Wallpaper," and Dad responded, "Fine. We just had a board meeting." He'd take out his old green American Express card and put it on the table.

We never had a formal board of directors in our business. I once tried to create a customer advisory board, in the hopes that it would afford us some insights into our customers' goals and their needs moving forward, so that we as a wholesale distributor would be in a better position to serve them. It ties into the old dictum from Ted Levitt of Harvard Business School, "In effective marketing, the goal is to give the customer what the customer wants." My father clearly thought it wasn't a great idea, but he encouraged me to go ahead and try it.

We brought in a dozen key customers. They sat around our conference room table and, while my goal was to get them to discuss their product needs for the future, it turned into what can best be described as a "bitching session." They complained about the cost of long-distance phone calls for placing orders, about handling charges, about pricing, and about return policies. I saw our bottom line disappearing and felt as though I was in a union meeting, and all the union wanted was "more." Though I did gain valuable information on the need for improved customer service, my goal was never achieved (as my dad anticipated). For me, the customer advisory board was a disaster; it was the first and the last. I simply wasn't ready to hear their input. See more in David's comments.

I've been fortunate to be a forum member through the Young Presidents' Organization and the World Presidents' Organization. The forum serves as my personal board of advisors, and though the composition has changed several times, the guidance and support of fellow members has helped me to make decisions around the hiring and firing of key executives, develop incentive compensation plans, refine marketing strategy, address family challenges and acquisitions and ultimately the sale of our business, and the launch of a new career. I can candidly say that other than my immediate family, the members of my forum have been my most intimate friends and the single most valuable source of support in my life.

DAVID'S PERSPECTIVE

As we've said, a CEO's job in the family business can be lonely, as both my father and I have experienced firsthand. Many CEOs understand that challenge, particularly in a family business, because the challenges you face as CEO are not confined to the business; they involve the family too and, as many CEOs of family businesses can attest, you're often the CEO of both the business and the family.

The big benefit of a board is to allow CEOs to have an organization they can bounce their ideas off. Knowing the value of boards is one of the reasons we created The Peer Alliance. Now we're considering a client advisory board for our own business, using past clients and others who understand our business to help support our growth. There's a lot of upside to that, but there are some risks associated with that as well. Remember Dad's disaster with his aborted customer advisory board? I think it goes back to the idea that if you're not ready to hear the input of others, you shouldn't have a board.

Many family businesses lack a formal board structure. One of the major reasons we started The Peer Alliance was because we saw a real opportunity to provide an environment in which current and emerging leaders could create and have the experience of a board for themselves—a "personal board of advisors" for the leaders in the family business to challenge them, to support them, to share their own experiences, and to explore opportunities at a deep level.

I'm also part of an organization called YAF, Young Adult Forum, children of YPOers, and it's a wonderful resource. I've been with these same people for ten years now. They've seen me through three different careers and have supported me and challenged me to go beyond what I would have accomplished without them. In many ways, that's what a board is all about: challenging the status quo. It's about looking for those opportunities that you might not necessarily see and pushing yourself in your organization, to strive beyond its current state. I think that's the benefit of a board at both the corporate as well as the personal level.

GUIDELINES FOR SUSTAINABILITY

- Compare a board of directors to an advisory board. Determine which works better for you.

- If a board of advisors isn't quite where you want to be, consider a peer group, such as The Peer Alliance. You don't have to go it alone.

- Consider term limits; avoid having too much "tweed" in the room.

- Compensate board members commensurate with perceived value.

- The boardroom isn't the kitchen table; set a boundary on family discussions.

- If you're not willing to prepare for board meetings, don't waste your time and that of others.

- Make sure that there are shareholder agreements and prenuptials that restrict the transfer of stock. It's important to protect the family enterprise and make sure that ex-spouses don't end up with enough shares to put a new spouse on the board.

- Match the board seats to the critical success factors of the business and the challenges of the family.

- Build a community in your board. Consider members' personalities and styles as well as technical knowledge.

- Stretch. Reach beyond your comfort zone. Boards can stimulate and support you. If you have a board, be sure you have a process to evaluate it.

- Share the warts and the moles. It's important that board members understand the inner dynamics of the business and the family.

- Dig deeper to learn more. There are hundreds of books that have been written just on governance, and the Internet offers boundless informational resources.

Chapter Eight

■ ▦ ■

The Succession of Leadership

The succession of leadership is a process, not an event. Research shows that sudden succession correlates with a greater risk of failure. Why? Sudden succession does not allow for a gradual increase and assessment of knowledge, responsibility, authority, decision making, or risk taking. Most important, it doesn't allow time for other stakeholders to gain the necessary respect for and trust of the candidate who's going through this learning process.

MAKE DECISIONS ON THE FUTURE OF LEADERSHIP BEFORE THE OLD MAN'S FUNERAL

We're frequently asked, "When should we start planning for leadership succession?" Our answer is one word: "*Now.*" The next-generation family members must be included in the process as much as possible because, ultimately, they are the ones who will have to live with the decisions.

It's clear that seniors won't let go until they're confident that their successors are ready to take hold. While the senior generation is currently running with the baton, the next-generation members must position themselves properly to take it. Once they have a firm grip on the baton, the senior generation will have an easier time letting go, knowing that the baton won't be dropped and the race won't be lost.

The typical tenure of a CEO in a family business is close to twenty years, more than double that of a nonfamily business. And while many family business CEOs love what they do, have a deep sense of stewardship, and are eager to train their successors, there are others who feel trapped. For them, it's a life sentence without parole.

Others fear a loss of identity or becoming irrelevant. They've been in control all their lives, and they're defined by what they do, so no matter how much they wish to exit, they will not do so until they feel they have something meaningful to do. Additionally, our experience shows that seniors won't let go until they're confident that their financial needs are going to be met.

Potential successors, meanwhile, must accept that having the right last name is not a criterion for leadership, and recognize that, like their entry, the succession of leadership is neither an entitlement nor an obligation but rather an opportunity to be earned. We increasingly see family businesses considering hiring nonfamily CEOs, some on an interim basis, charged with mentoring the next generation while running the business.

For many next-gens, taking over the family business might seem like imprisonment as well. We've helped numerous clients deal with this. We've offered some "get out of jail free" opportunities to exit the business without ego or financial compromise, rather than to lead it into the next generation. For some, taking that option was a tremendous relief. Others were too fearful of change and wouldn't let go. In one instance, a CEO paid his son $1 million a year to stay home. Another son was tired of the business, never really liked it in the first place, and only took over to please his parents. He wanted to get out but couldn't. He had golden handcuffs, and his wife would not allow the exit—too much of a blow to her position in the community, let alone the financial consequences.

The Curran Insurance Group is a second-generation family business in the commercial insurance industry where Dad's good intentions didn't quite succeed. The father, Ben, built the business from the ground up and for many years was the primary revenue driver, a powerful, strong personality. Over the last five years, he brought his daughter, Judy, into the business, along with another woman, Candice, who had previous insurance sales experience and was a strong producer. Although Ben never wanted to admit it, deep down he knew he needed to bring Candice into the business to help his daughter eventually run the company and lead their twenty-five agents. Judy was not passionate about the business and thus had little to no desire to assume a leadership position. She was quite content with having her father and Candice be the rainmakers while she devoted most of her time to riding horses and working a few insurance cases on the side.

Ben was referred to us by his attorney and asked if we could work with the family to create a leadership succession strategy that would position Judy and Candice to run the business together as partners. We spent time with Ben, Judy, and Candice to experience their personalities and styles and learn their desires, concerns, and expectations. We explored different scenarios, including roles and responsibilities, decision-making authority, and ownership in the business, but the main challenge was whether Candice was willing to be responsible for driving the future of the business while partnered with someone who was only in it because of the lifestyle it provided and the limited accountability that came with the job.

In the end, Ben was never able to have a candid conversation with Judy, for fear of repercussions from her as well as his wife, who would never allow the grandchildren to be held hostage. As a result, Candice made the difficult decision to part ways, head west, and start her own business. Ben and Judy still work together, but nothing has really changed other than that Ben is a few years older and no closer to retirement.

On the path to success, Driscoll Manufacturing is a third-generation family business led by Mary, the daughter of the founder. She has two children in the business: a son, Saul, and a daughter, Michelle—both of whom are in their early thirties. Saul has been in the business for five years and Michelle for three. They are bright, hard working, and appreciative of the opportunity that is in front of them. After participating in an intergenerational workshop we delivered, the Driscolls hired us to create a leadership development plan for Saul and Michelle. Although both are doing well in the business, it was not clear as to what their paths would be or which of them (if either) would assume the reins of the business. Through the initial interviews and 360 Performance Appraisals, it was evident that both Saul and Michelle had some areas that needed attention, particularly in their relationship as brother and sister partners in the business and regarding their management styles—nothing terribly alarming but rather a refining and enhancing that would better position both to ultimately drive the business together.

We guided the siblings as they created a professional development plan and shared it with their mother and the senior management team. They embraced the coaching and consulting process as we helped them to unravel past issues that were standing in the way of their relationship with one another. Now they're communicating better as partners, have incorporated a collaborative approach to working with other leaders, and have received support for new initiatives they want to implement. At the same time, Mary, Saul, and Michelle have developed a long-term plan that will position both children to assume leadership positions in the business and ultimately sustain it for another generation.

Here's a case that's a work in progress. Bruno Vlansk's father started the Vlansk Weaving Company sixty-five years ago and has been running it since his father died. Bruno is type C—rather passive but keen on detail—and brought his two sons, Oliver and Don, into the business over the last fifteen years. We were asked to facilitate design of a leadership transition plan to pass the business from Bruno to his sons.

But the sons don't see eye to eye on how the business should be run. Oliver has outstanding technical skills and industry knowledge but also has an abrasive personality, known for his abundance of offensive comments. Don is in and out of the factory, pursuing unrelated interests. Bruno requires no accountability, and there are no consequences for Oliver and Don's comportment. There is also massive triangulation among the three, where neither son is capable of candidly addressing issues directly with the other. All communication between Oliver and Don is funneled through Bruno, thus putting him in a very difficult position. He is completely conflict averse, unable to manage the dynamic between his sons, and fears that the relationship between the two could get openly contentious.

Although ostensibly we were hired to help facilitate a plan for leadership transition, Bruno really brought us on hoping we would deliver his tough message: that his sons needed to get their act together and figure out if they want to take over this business or not. He isn't about to hand over the family business he worked his life to develop, only to have his kids destroy it. Serving as the messenger, however, is not our role. In our experience, being the messengers is the quickest way to end an engagement because if the recipients don't like the message, we end up getting shot.

Much of our work with Bruno and his sons is focused on creating an environment in which they can communicate effectively with one another, learn to have difficult conversations without being difficult, and address personality and commitment issues, validating each other and hearing each other without judgment and without defensiveness.

Like so many challenges facing business families, all of the difficult issues are interrelated. In this case, the lack of guidelines and clarity regarding behavior and commitment to the business combined with their personalities and styles. Although Oliver was given the title of president, he was never truly anointed, because Bruno recognizes the challenges with Oliver's personality, style, and total lack of emotional intelligence. Bruno's inability to relinquish control is exacerbated by his fears that giving control to Oliver would make Don feel less loved. He is treating his sons like "children," not like business partners, and that gets in the way of building a sustainable family business. In families, it's about unconditional love, but in business, we must judge people on their knowledge, skill, and experience and on what they do and how well they do it, not on who they are, and that's where this family is conflicted. Even though Don is too wrapped up in his personal life to carry his weight, his father isn't up to the task of telling him so, which means the ultimate consequence—being fired—doesn't exist in this business. Until family members are willing to be truly candid with one another and commit performance standards with accountability and consequences, there is little we can do to help with a plan for leadership succession.

Successful transition of leadership is also about understanding the needs of the senior generation, as in a case from several years ago. In this case, on the surface, the senior generation's needs were sharing and transparency. As the New York City business was being transitioned from a mother to her son when Mom was in Florida, she wanted reports on how the business was doing. No matter how much information he provided, the son told us, she wanted more. So we coined the word "hyperinfomate," and encouraged the son to send Mom more information than she could possibly handle. The real issue, of course, was not about information. It was about control, and beneath control was the issue of trust. Mom wasn't convinced that her son could handle the business. The son's preparation, communication of abundant information, and his demonstration of transparency had the intended impact. When Mom saw that her son had everything under control, her trust and confidence in him grew. She was better able to let go and no longer needed those copious reports.

Here's another example of successful succession. Steve Grossman, the former chair of the Democratic National Committee and former treasurer of the Commonwealth of Massachusetts, followed the path of his grandfather in successfully grooming his two sons, David and Ben, to be fourth-generation leaders in an enterprise that early on recognized the impact of electronic communication and morphed from the Massachusetts Envelope Company to Grossman Marketing Group. Like his grandfather before him, who dropped the keys on his son's desk to be a one-dollar-a-year man for Franklin Delano Roosevelt in the 1940s, Steve dropped his keys on his sons' desks to enter public service and another career that brings personal fulfillment. David and Ben have been trained and anointed and successfully serve as well-aligned copresidents.

David and Ben have been in the business for many years and have gone through rotations in every department. They've been on the road. They've been in the back room running printing presses. They know the business inside out and backward. They also established a healthy and stable relationship with one another and have complementary skills and know how to manage disagreements.

This is a family that communicates openly, candidly, and respectfully. They've mastered the skills of transition. David and Ben proved their competence, giving Steve the confidence in his sons, allowing him to enjoy a rewarding new life post politics in the world of philanthropy with no fear that either his identity or the business will be lost.

PAUL'S PERSPECTIVE

My transition to leadership in our family business was a gradual and certain escalation over a number of years. I learned the business basics and how to communicate more effectively, how to build on the remarks of others, how to gain allies, and how to be the last one to speak in a meeting, and, after a reasonable number of mistakes and demonstrating sufficient ability, was steadily empowered by my dad.

Early on, we wanted to expand territory into the state of Connecticut, which required submitting an extensive proposal to our supplier, Borden Chemical Company. We needed the demographics, a marketing plan, and a compelling argument explaining why we would do a better job than the present distributor, and my dad asked me to put it all together. I did, and we succeeded in gaining the expanded territory. Likewise, before we made acquisitions in New York and Pennsylvania, my dad tasked me with crunching the numbers, doing the *pro formas,* and creating marketing plans and plans to integrate staff into the culture of our current organization. My dad gave me the responsibility of leading our branch operations. I'm proud I didn't let him down. More and more, I learned the intricacies of our business, worked to build a team and reinforced the confidence my dad already had in me.

When we went to the bank to borrow money to finance the expanded inventory in Philadelphia, though personal guarantees were not required, the banker handed my dad the note to sign, and he passed it to me. I asked why, and he said, "Because I never want you to forget the meaning of debt." He then made a copy of that note and ensconced it in bronze, mounted it on a walnut plaque, and hung it on the side of the wall next to my desk, right above my telephone. He wanted me to see it every day.

My dad supported my involvement both in the Young Presidents' Organization and in going through the OPM Program at Harvard Business School, recognizing both as professional development.

He also supported my termination of one of his earliest hires—one of the most important employees in the company who was unable to be a team player. When the board (Dad and me) appointed me president and CEO, Dad wrote a press release and sent it to customers, suppliers, local papers, and trade associations. Though it felt like a coronation, I was a bit ill at ease. I remember telling my dad that I didn't have all the answers. He replied, "You don't have to know the answers to everything, you just have to know how to find the answers to everything." As he was retiring, he supported my bringing in a COO to run the day-to-day operations of the business to leave me free for strategy and planning, no doubt anticipating my desire to explore other pursuits as well.

To me, the most remarkable ascension to leadership occurred the day after my father died. We were on our way to a memorial service when a man suddenly ran across the street and hit my car, knocking off the passenger mirror, diving across the hood, and landing on the street. I pulled over immediately and went to the man. He stood up and said he was okay. He was just running across the street and didn't see my car. A nearby mounted police officer rode over to take charge of the situation. I was looking at my watch. We were late for the service. The man told the officer that he was okay. He didn't need an ambulance. The officer said to me, "I want your license and registration."

I said, "But he said he's okay."

He angrily repeated, "I want your license and registration!"

When I told him I was going to be late to my father's memorial service, he told me, "Don't worry. Let your family go. I'll take you to the service."

I lost it a little: "What are you going to do, take me there on your friggin' horse?" (And I didn't say "friggin'.")

The cop looked at me and said, "One more word out of your mouth, and I'm going to take you in." David was standing right next to me. He leaned in and said, "Dad, I need to talk to you." I turned toward him and looked up. He put his hands on my shoulders and said, "Dad, you're out of control. Let me handle this."

I looked up into his eyes, and calmly said, "Okay."

I stepped aside, and David and the police officer had a further conversation. David came back to me and said, "You go. It's okay. I'll take care of this." At that moment, for me, my son was a man and a leader. Even though he was twenty, he'd always been my kid to me. But now, seeing him calmly, resolutely take charge, I listened to him like I had never listened to him before.

In our business, David's vision is broader than mine. He sees the future of our practice; he has proven his competency, and it was easy for me to relinquish the CEO role. He's progressed steadily, and as he takes hold, my letting go is very easy. Another thing that's made it easy is his deep concern for me and my future and our ability to talk frankly about it. Knowing how deeply he cares makes it infinitely easier.

DAVID'S PERSPECTIVE

For me, moving to a leadership position was a much different experience than it had been for my dad. Because I didn't come into the family business until I was thirty-nine, a lot of my leadership growth was through other avenues and in other businesses. Part of it was through advanced education, with both a master's in counseling and an MBA, and taking multiple leadership courses at a large Fortune 100 company where I had spent eight years.

My growth required actively seeking out leadership opportunities, as well as coming to understand my skill set with assessments and from coaching. Much of it was through mentoring by my father to move into a leadership role in my own right.

One of the more powerful things happened when I was working at EMC, a large Fortune 100 company. I was working under a great manager with whom I was friendly, a gentleman I really admired. I had gone after a high-level position and didn't get it, and I was deeply disappointed. When I went to talk to him about it, he was quite blunt with me, saying, "You didn't get it, because there was a sense that you weren't ready for that position." He shared with me something that I still look at every single day when I'm in my office, a poem called "The Man in the Glass" by Dale Wimbrow (see addendum #18), a poem about being honest with yourself, which ends with this stanza:

> You can fool the whole world down the pathway of years,
> And get pats on the back as you pass,
> But your final reward will be heartaches and tears
> If you've cheated the man in the glass.

For me to be truly honest with myself and understand my real skill set, I had to look in the mirror and ask, "What do I really want?" It was a powerful moment for me and affirmed my career working with business families—to work with my dad, to make a difference in the lives of others. I've shared this poem many times over the years, particularly with the younger generation, because I was there once, too. In order to become a true leader, you must be honest with yourself, you must know your strengths and your limitations, and you must know how to manage around them.

When I joined my dad, I'd already had leadership positions in other companies. My father felt that it was important for us to truly be partners in this venture; I was never going to work for him, I was going to work with him. Consequently, we structured our roles and responsibilities to be those of partners. From day one, my father truly anointed me in the position of president of the organization. Although we talk about them because I value his opinion, he empowered me to make decisions on operational areas of the business. And he's able to "let go," which is painfully difficult for many in the senior generation. I think it's a combination of the field that we are in and also his confidence that I'm able to make the right decisions and drive the business forward.

I also feel that my dad is at the point in his career where he's earned the right to do whatever he wants in the company, in terms of the amounts of time, energy, and the areas of the business that he wants to focus on. And I know that the two areas that my father is truly passionate about and which are his areas of expertise are in the consulting area and writing. I was glad to take on the rest of the job of running the company because it was a great way for me to learn the entire business and, again, to position us for sustainability.

My dad now uses the title of "founder," and I serve as president and CEO, and we have instituted a transition of leadership that has been a graceful process over the preceding seven years. We're strongly positioned for the long term because we did it methodically, we did it over time, and we did it together, conscious also that we had to model for our clients the right way to go about it.

GUIDELINES FOR SUSTAINABILITY

- The succession of leadership is a process and not an event; plan for it well in advance of the need.

- Create a plan for leadership transition clearly addressing the needs of the business, the desires of the family, and the competencies and areas of interest of the next generation.

- Talk about what seniors need in order to let go of control and what is required of the next generation to take up the reins.

- Be sure that the seniors have a meaningful next role and are financially secure.

- The right last name doesn't guarantee a leadership role.

- Have open and honest conversations about the future of the business with members of the younger generation.

- Position the next-generation members to succeed by exploring their strengths and limitations.

- Next-gens need to make their own mark; that may mean a change in direction.

- Consider a 360 Performance Appraisal (anonymous feedback from peers, supervisors, and direct reports compared to self-perceptions).

- Look at the needs of the business, and compare them to the competencies of emerging leaders. This is a valuable tool to help next-gens understand what they need to learn to assure a smooth transition. (See Addendum #12: Attributes of Leadership© Checklist.)

- Value self-awareness, personality, style, and emotional intelligence over technical industry knowledge.

- Obtain clarity on roles and decision-making authority.

- "Look in the glass." Honestly assess yourself.

- Next-gens: prove your competence.

- Attention, seniors: seek the opportunity to anoint the next generation once the mantle of leadership has been earned.

Chapter Nine

■ ■ ■

The Transition of Ownership

The transition of ownership is complex. The diverse stories and intricate questions call for the guidance and support of multiple professionals. Many family businesses have a team consisting of attorney, accountant, insurance advisor, valuation experts, investment banker, and more.

FREE ASSOCIATION YIELDS A FEW QUESTIONS

Whose needs get met—those of the senior generation, those of the next generation, or those of the business? Does ownership only transition to family members? How do you define "family members"? Can shares go to spouses? What if the spouse remarries? Are you okay with his or her second spouse driving around in the Mercedes for which you worked your tail off? Remember the story in chapter 7 about the fellow whose wife ended up with enough stock to put her second husband on the board?

How about an ESOP (employee stock ownership plan)? And what about the children? Are shares gifted or sold, or a combination of the two, and do they go only to those children working in the business or to all children? Do they go equally or in differing percentages? Are we talking about voting stock or nonvoting stock, and does the stock go only to children in the family bloodline? What about adopted children? Then, of course, there are the grandchildren. We know a family where the grandfather gifted so much stock to his grandchildren that his son resented the fact that his kids were wealthier than he was. Further, there's the topic of business valuation. Should it be at fair market value? And with or without a discount for minority interest?

The complications, ramifications, and implications abound. In one instance, a family team successfully bought out the interests of eighty-one other family members. Another fourth-generation family has ownership dispersed among six siblings and their fifteen children, with a voting trust giving decision-making control to the CEO. And there's the dad who gave the business to his kids—but kept the real estate, with no written lease. The kids sold the business and the new owner decided to move, so Dad's left with an empty building in a not-so-desirable part of town. And on and on and on. Then there are other families that end up in court for years, and the only winners are the attorneys.

UNANSWERED QUESTIONS CREATE CONFUSION AND CHAOS

Inadequate planning or avoiding the discussion of ownership succession leaves these questions unanswered and fails to protect the family and the business. It would require multiple volumes to present all the possible ways that the transition of ownership can play out—but let's examine a few, just to get an idea.

We'll start with Ron and Irene, a brother and sister, fifty-fifty business partners who had been working on a shareholders' agreement for a couple of years. We were told they just put off signing it as other matters took priority. Together they made a successful team, but Irene died unexpectedly and, according to her will, since there were no restrictions on the stock certificates, her shares went to her husband, Leon. Ron and Leon's relationship was cordial until Leon told Ron that he wanted to occupy Irene's office and take over her role as CFO in the business. That's when Ron called us.

One family has a common way of pruning the family tree. One of four siblings, all equal partners, died and his stock was redeemed by the corporation from his estate with life insurance and redistributed among the remaining partners. In this arrangement, he who lives longest wins.

Then there are stories of how an ill-planned transition sank one founder's future. Stan, who'd built a highly successful chain of carpet stores, had one child, Thomas, who joined him in the business after college. Stan decided to retire on his sixty-fifth birthday and to complete the transfer of the business ownership to Thomas, never retaining voting control. His simple unwritten agreement with Thomas involved a payout consisting of his current salary and perks for the next twenty years. The numbers were easy for Thomas, as the business was quite profitable and could comfortably support both families.

One year later, Thomas divorced and remarried a woman addicted to spending, so Thomas drew ever-larger sums from the business. When there was a downturn in the economy and business revenue suffered, cash flow became tight. The situation worsened over the next couple of years, and a once-profitable, successful enterprise filed for bankruptcy. Stan's income ceased, and his stock portfolio tanked. Now Stan, in his seventies, is working as a salesman in a competitor's store.

"FAIR" DOESN'T ALWAYS MEAN "EQUAL"

Charlie and Emily Collins were refining their estate plans when they met with their three children in their forties, only one of whom worked in the business. The other two had successful independent careers. Charlie and Emily had always treated their children equally, so they were inclined to do the same with stock in their business. Jerry, the son who had worked in the business for twenty years and was responsible for much of its growth, was enraged. His siblings said he was paid a salary for those years of work, and since the ownership was still in the hands of their parents, and since the parents always treated their children equally, why should this be any different? That's when our phone rang.

We helped the family evaluate what the business was worth *before* Jerry made a significant contribution. That amount was split in thirds. Next, the average value of the business was determined for the years that Jerry was *de facto* acting as his father's partner. Charlie and Emily agreed one-half of that average was to be Jerry's for his sweat equity, and the remaining half would be divided, with one-third going to each of the children. While Charlie, Emily, and Jerry saw this as fair, the other two siblings were still grumbling that, in a business, fair does not always mean equal.

In another case, Martin and Arnold were brothers with an outstanding business relationship for many years. Martin had one son and Arnold had two, and when it came time to transition the business to the next generation, while they accounted for prior retained earnings and divided them appropriately between the two partners, they opted to transition the ownership of the company in an atypical way. The choice, obviously, could have been Martin's to transition his 50 percent equity to his son, Kevin. Arnold, accordingly, could also have transitioned his 50 percent interest, giving 25 percent to each of his sons.

Martin, with obvious support and encouragement from Arnold and his sons, decided there would be a greater harmony among the three future partners if they each had an equal stake in the business. Martin's son, Kevin, understood and supported that decision, giving up, in fact, a significant portion of his birthright for the sake of better business harmony with his cousins. (We always wondered what would have happened if Arnold had four or five or more children.)

We've also run into situations where two equal owners decided they could no longer work with one another. We worked with two brothers who owned a retail store fifty-fifty. They were in their early sixties and had been working with each other for about thirty-five years. Their relationship was "comfortable," but they came to the conclusion that they no longer wanted to continue to work together and weren't sure what to do, so they hired us to help them clarify their individual goals and decide how to move forward. Both of them were open to buying the other out, but the question was how to do it fairly.

We recommended a "Texas Shootout." We took out a coin, flipped it, and explained, "The winner of the coin toss can set the price and the terms of the deal, then the other one can choose whether he wants to be the buyer or the seller at that price and under those terms."

This way, the brother who set the price and the terms had to do it fairly. For instance, let's assume one brother said, "I want $50 million, and I want it in cash today," then the other brother could say, "Fine. Then I'll sell." The Texas Shootout ensures fairness.

The buyer subsequently brought his son in to help run the business. The brothers have frequent dinners together and spend holidays together and have a better relationship than ever before. What potentially could have been a highly conflicted situation worked out fairly for both sides.

One family's advance planning really paid off at transition time. Will Hanson owned the company, had two nephews in business, and, with no children of his own, was looking to transition both the ownership and leadership to them. He created a five-year ownership transition plan: over time, he transitioned the equity position, while he retained voting rights. When Uncle Will's equity interest was no longer significant, he transitioned the voting control to his nephews. He gifted slowly to lessen the tax consequence and was able to do so, taking significant discounts. He retained control until he no longer felt at risk and it was appropriate to let go. Will is now enjoying life as a golfer, an artist, and a traveler.

Decisions around the future of ownership are complex indeed. There is, perhaps, no single topic, if this could even be called a single topic, that is more important than protecting the family and the business with thoughtful planning.

PAUL'S PERSPECTIVE

After several years working with my dad, he gifted 49 percent of the business to me. At that time, its value was relatively low, and 49 percent as minority interest carried a significant discount. Several years later, he gifted me an additional 2 percent, also at a minority discount. Ultimately, he gifted me the remaining 49 percent of the business, which again carried a significant discount. This was a tax-efficient way to do it, and the business was recapitalized. Be sure to check with your financial professional. Tax laws have since changed, and that is no longer quite so easy to accomplish, but it was effective at that time. While graciously accepting these gifts, I was concerned about my brother and "fairness," and my dad assured me my brother was appropriately taken care of, having used a formula similar to that of the Collins family.

My dad was able to let go of the business gracefully because his financial needs were secure, he was confident in me, and he had something else in his life to move on to. He was a talented artist, involved the philanthropic community, and had interests in life beyond the business. Even though he started the wholesale distribution end of the business, and it was in many ways his baby, it was clearly not his identity, and he was able to let go. So it was, fortunately, a successful experience.

In our desire to model best practices and guidelines for sustainability, David and I have created a comprehensive shareholder agreement. As much as I love my daughter-in-law and David loves his mom, neither one of us wishes to be in a business partnership with either one. Thus, there's clarity on conditions under which our stock would transfer from one to the other based on illness, incapacity, or death. We've covered our bases, and that is perhaps the single most important document the business can have. When I soon transition the ownership of my half of our business to David (and still continue with client consulting), the only condition I'll put on it is that he continues to refer to the business as "ours."

DAVID'S PERSPECTIVE

I was welcomed into our business similar to the way in which my father had been a generation earlier. He knew it was important for me to feel that we were equals and partners, and because I was coming in with the right credentials at age thirty-nine and not twenty-five, I had truly earned the right to be partners with him. He dissolved his current corporation, and together we started a new corporation as fifty-fifty partners. That's when he gave me that stock certificate etched in glass.

We do not recommend this to other families since, as equals, if we are in a deadlock we don't have a way to resolve it. Yet both of us felt confident enough in our relationship with each other and ability to communicate effectively to structure it that way. Frankly, if we can't figure out how to work through a deadlock, then we have no business consulting to other families and working with them on communication. In the seven years that we've worked together, it has never been an issue, and I think that success is due to the fact that my dad and I share the same goals for the business and for one another personally, and we talk about them and reaffirm them often. Partly, too, it's where he is in his life; being a member of the senior generation, he's kind of "been there, done that." He sees in me the future of the business, and he's comfortable with that. The plan is working well for us.

Typically, when we think of ownership, there are two aspects to consider. Is it about control, or is it about money? In our case, as a consulting organization, there are really no retained earnings, so ownership isn't about money. Ownership in our business, as it is in many businesses, is truly about control, and Dad had no issue relinquishing control to me. By the same token, any major decision that we make, we make together. It's a testament to the importance of great communication, and to the trust between us, that it works so well.

GUIDELINES FOR SUSTAINABILITY

- Create a shareholder agreement. It's the single most important document you can have to protect yourself, your family, and your business.

- Engage the best advisors from appropriate disciplines. The process is complex.

- Communicate; it is the key to success. The conversation about ownership transition should be done well ahead of the event. Don't put it off. Sign the documents.

- Be sure there is clarity on whose needs are being met.

- Understand the differing goals of the multiple owners for the transition of their shares. Sometimes it's about voting control. Sometimes it's about money and the value of the business.

- Think prudently about the unintended short-term and long-term consequences of well-intentioned present decisions. Discuss how the ownership will be passed. By gifting? By selling? By a combination of the two? There is no right or wrong answer here; it's really what works for the family, and every family is different. Many seniors believe the next generation should have some "skin in the game" and want their children to purchase some of the equity.

- Accept that fair doesn't always mean equal, and equal isn't always fair.

- Be sure the financial needs of parents are met. If current owners fear financial jeopardy, then they're going to have a hard time letting go. In many cases, the value of the business is the owners' "retirement plan," and they need to know they'll be able to continue living the life they've been working so hard to create.

- Retain the voting stock until you no longer feel at financial risk.

- Be clear on a process for business valuation.

- Be cautious and reflective about voting control. Be sure to create a structure that does not allow for a deadlock situation where the business and family have no means of resolution.

- Explore alternative funding mechanisms. There's a whole menu of opportunities for creative financing between traditional debt, life insurance, investment bankers, or an interim third-party investor, etc.

Chapter Ten

■ ▨ ■

When It's Time to Sell

Sometimes the sale of the family business is best for the family, and sometimes it's best for the business. Perhaps the business has peaked and the owners receive an offer they simply can't refuse. Maybe there's no heir apparent. Maybe there's a family battle that can't be resolved. Perhaps other opportunities present a greater return on investment, or there are compelling family needs.

Sustainability isn't just about continuity of a family business, it's also about the continuity of family history, culture, values, and wealth. Sale of a family business isn't necessarily a failure. It may allow for investment in other ventures that provide even greater reward to the stakeholders, both materially and personally. Owners have multiple options: liquidation; sale to a competitor, a private equity firm, or venture capitalists; an ESOP; and even adopting an heir. The sale of a family business can be stressful. We know of the funeral director who died the day of the closing.

The Lockhart family was in its third generation, with six family principals in their fifties who all had the identical compensation and perks, regardless of roles. An MIT guru urged them to sell ahead of the anticipated entry of fourteen G4s because they refused to alter the culture (pay and perk equality for all, no matter what the role in the business), and the business simply couldn't grow fast enough to support the incoming generation. One branch acquired the family's investment portfolio and has grown it exponentially for the benefit of all. Simply stated, it was time for the business to serve the family.

But the choice isn't always that cut and dried. Earl is seventy-four years old and has worked in his family's business for fifty years. The business needs cash to grow and relocate to larger quarters, but Earl is tired, has some health issues, and feels it's time to sell. Several investment bankers interested in helping him out with a liquidity event have approached him, but Earl has mixed emotions. What about his son and daughter, who both work in the business? Though neither has the ability to take it over, they both enjoy comfortable salaries and perks. The business has been Earl's identity, and though he'd like to cash out, he's concerned not only for his children but also for his long-term, dedicated employees.

When we spoke with Earl, it was evident that he was battling between emotion and reason. As discussions ensued, we helped Earl to craft sale criteria. These included employment provisions for his son and daughter and key nonfamily employees, a three-year advisory contract for himself, preservation of his family history by any acquirer, purchase of the company's real estate, and, of course, release of the New England Patriots season tickets to Earl.

As we helped Earl develop his plan, he became increasingly comfortable with the idea of a sale. We linked him up to a valuation expert and an investment banker with experience in this field, helped him set up a family bank and a charitable gift fund, and held his hand through the acquisition process. The emotional support enabled rational decision making for the benefit of all.

We were told the story of the late George Murray, who founded and built a business more than seventy years ago and was advised to gift his stock to his five children and ten grandchildren. The goal was to minimize taxes. There was a provision that family members working in the business could buy out the others at a formula based on book value. Over the next two generations, the business grew substantially, and no one exercised the option.

Fast-forward to two generations with seventy-five stockholders in the business run by two of George's grandsons who opted to exercise their right to buy out the other stockholders. Two years later, the two grandsons chose to sell the business to a Fortune 500 company. Though this was not their intent when they bought out other family members, the prior stockholders were furious, as the price was eight times what they had been paid. In the absence of a clawback (an agreement that would have provided the prior stockholders with a proportionate return), the family was in turmoil. Lawyers were involved, suits were threatened, and the sons, in an attempt to preserve family relationships, offered a settlement, but resentment lingered for many years. Moral of the story: think about both short-term and long-term consequences of a decision; consider a clawback. And, once again, don't let the tax tail wag the dog.

An accountant friend shared the story of Carl and Donna, both in their late thirties, who took over their parents' art gallery after their dad retired. Carl handled the operational side of the business—bookkeeping, personnel, and property management—whereas Donna, who was a talented artist herself, managed artist relations, exhibits, and special events. To the outside world, Donna was the face of the business. Carl and Donna's relationship was solid until Donna's relationship with a landscape architect blossomed and Donna decided to leave the business and join her new beau running a garden center. In Carl's mind, he was left "high and dry," with no one to replace her. Distraught, bitter, and angry, he sold the gallery for a fraction of its worth, just to get out.

We worked on a case with two sisters, both in their sixties, who were approached by a competitor to purchase their small chain of furniture stores. Their mother, now in her nineties, had gifted the business, founded by her father, to her daughters many years previously. When, on previous occasions, the sisters had mentioned a possible sale to their mother, her response had been a flat, "Over my dead body." Understandably, when this competitor came to them with an offer to buy them out, they were hesitant to bring it up with Mother.

That's when we were called in and asked to facilitate a family meeting. Mom was informed that the meeting had been arranged to discuss family business issues and planning for the future. After interviewing each family member individually, it became clear that Mom's resistance to selling the business was indeed a challenge the sisters needed to overcome.

We helped the sisters and their mother to achieve alignment on some specific goals: preservation of family history, relationships and values, happiness, and preservation of wealth. We then brainstormed ways in which these could be attained. When the option of a sale came up, Mom became silent, but her eyes filled up with tears. With our expression of empathy, Mom was encouraged to share her feelings, not something she would typically do.

She spoke emotionally of her father and how he struggled to start the business, surviving the Great Depression and then moving forward. She said that the mere thought of a sale made her feel disloyal to his memory. We encouraged Mom to seek some counseling and support around her feelings for her father, which she reluctantly agreed to do. The sisters decided to hold off for the moment on further discussions about the future.

About three months later, we were called back to continue the brainstorming. Mom was better able to let go of her own emotional attachment and focus on her daughters and their needs for the future. Reflecting upon their agreed-upon goals, she now saw that the sale of the business was a valid option.

The Harris brothers owned several tire and automotive shops. Both in their late fifties, with other interests in mind and no apparent successors, they were considering the sale of their business. We had been working with them off and on around a variety of matters and were called in to help plan an exit strategy.

We explained to the brothers that, just as the first thing to do when contemplating the sale of a car is to have it detailed, the same applies to the business. Working with their accountant, we recommended a series of steps, including removing the inactive sister, cousin, and one mother-in-law from the payroll. Four company-owned Mercedes were purchased from the business by the brothers for themselves and their wives, as was the company-owned condominium in a ski resort in New Hampshire. Country club membership and credit card use were curtailed, as were grooming services for the mother-in-law's Afghan hound. Computer systems were updated, and a better system for control of cash sales was implemented. Financial statements were recast, and after two years, the earnings multiple was substantial, and it was time to talk with the experts in mergers and acquisitions.

PAUL'S PERSPECTIVE

As mentioned in chapter 7, when the wallcovering industry peaked and consumption declined, we knew we were in for dramatic change. We hired an expert in strategic planning and gathered our key staff for an off-site retreat to brainstorm options. Much to my surprise, one option that emerged was the sale of the business.

As the sole stockholder at that point, the decision was mine. Consulting with my dad, who had retired by that time, and our trusted advisor (who became the chief negotiator), I knew that a sale was the best option, as I didn't have sufficient confidence in the industry to risk further investment. But I clearly had mixed emotions. Our daughter and son were still in college, and I would be denying them the opportunity that was given to me. I also wanted to protect the key people in our organization who had helped build the business. And what about our family legacy? Still, the sale of the business would mean that I'd be free to pursue my real passion in the field of education.

As I was contemplating the sale of the business, I called on a dear friend, Barrie Greiff, formerly psychiatrist to Harvard Business School, and told him I needed a sanity check. When he asked why, I said, "I'm thinking of selling our family business."

He said, "You do need a sanity check. Come on in." I entered his office. It didn't have the stereotypical black couch. Ironically, my lower back, which has been troublesome for years, was in excruciating pain. So I actually ended up lying down on the floor of his office, sharing my thoughts and feelings about the sale of the business.

When Barrie had heard me out, he suggested, "Go back to graduate school. Go pursue your education. Explore. See what comes next."

I asked him, "Where are you heading with this?"

His response was, "If you don't know where you're going, you'll never let go of where you've been." (That's a line we repeatedly share, with attribution to Barrie, of course.) After consummating the sale of the business, I took his advice to heart, took the necessary aptitude test, applied, and was accepted into a graduate program where I was older than most of my professors. That invigorating experience served as a catalyst to the launch of a second career.

Back to the sale. After meeting with two potential suitors, we chose one and negotiated a sale, and within eight months, in an anxious and euphoric moment, closed on the transaction. Throughout, I had tremendous support from my parents, my wife, and our son and daughter. They understood the risk associated with continuing the business and my desire to follow my passion; I was still young enough in my midforties to take this leap of faith. I did so with their blessing, which was a tremendous support. And though many times buyers and sellers experience remorse, I felt a sense of freedom unlike one I hadn't had in many years, and it was exhilarating.

DAVID'S PERSPECTIVE

When my dad sold our family business, I was still too young to have given much consideration to the idea of going into it myself, so the sale was a nonissue for me. I supported it because it was going to allow Dad to go off to pursue other passions he had been long waiting to explore. Unlike many situations where kids may be hesitant to see their parents sell the business because it's where they'd intended to make their own careers, neither my sister nor I had those concerns. For my father, although it was unquestionably the right time to sell, return to school, and explore other options, I know there was a part of him that was feeling bad about giving up the family business where he'd so enjoyed working with his own father. Of course, we didn't know Transition Consulting Group was going to exist, and we certainly didn't know I was going to work in it twenty-five years later.

When you sell a family business, one question arises, what does the family do with the assets? Many times, they start or invest in one or more businesses and become a "family enterprise," and/or create a family office and a charitable fund and pursue philanthropic initiatives. Shortly after the sale of Dad's business, we considered buying a summer camp for our family to run together. We all thoroughly enjoyed our summer camp experiences, and we talked together about how that might work and the roles we'd have. Dad performed due diligence and the numbers looked right, but my sister and I were still too young to really commit ourselves, so we passed.

Dad moved on, completed graduate studies, got connected with Northeastern University, helped launch and run its Center for Family Business, and started consulting. Jody and I had our own independent careers, so the concept of a family business took a hiatus for a number of years. Mom and Dad invested wisely and created a family charitable fund in which we're involved.

GUIDELINES FOR SUSTAINABILITY

- Consider that a sale is sometimes about more than the business; it's about preserving the family's history, culture, values, and wealth.

- Determine if it's appropriate for the business to serve the family.

- Protect family and key nonfamily executives to the extent you can.

- Consider both short-term and long-term consequences.

- Manage the emotions of family members, including those in the business, those who were in the business, and even those who might have been in the business, because the family business can be so enmeshed with the family identity, and emotion will trump logic every time.

- Don't let the tax tail wag the dog. Sometimes it makes sense to make decisions for tax purposes, but consider the longer-term implications.

- Detail the business. Get Aunt Nellie off the payroll.

- Find your passion and pursue it.

- Provide a safe environment in which to have open, candid, and honest conversations around the potential of selling the family business; listen to all family members' points of view. Validating each person's point of view is critical to building alignment as to what the decision ultimately will be.

- Have someone hold your hand in the process. It's okay to bring in someone who might have superior skills to do the negotiating for you.

- Be willing to let go of the past, live in the present, and look to the future.

Chapter Eleven

■ ▨ ■

Communication

There are more than one billion Google links to "communication." Maybe this book will be one more! In our experience, ineffective communication lies at the core of every relationship issue, challenge, dilemma, perceived failure, and conflict in a family enterprise. Poor communication leads to inaccurate assumptions and can limit or destroy relationships, prevent alignment by the family on strategy and the direction of the future of the business, and ultimately impact the sustainability of the family enterprise—and even the family.

We've seen poor communication manifest itself in a variety of ways. Styles can vary from culture to culture and family to family. There's the father banging on the table and screaming, "I never, ever hit one of my kids"; plus the daughter who told us she knew her father was furious when he dropped his jaw one quarter of an inch; the son who flew across the dinner table attempting to choke his father; or the father, whose way of communicating parental control was by having an indiscreet relationship with his son's girlfriend. And what about the two brothers in business together who haven't exchanged a single word in six years, yet the business is doing well. These are all true stories, hard as they are to believe.

There are some relationships that may take months and even years to work out, including long periods of pain, reflection, and silence. Others are so fractured they may not be repairable. Curiously, as distressing as it may be to accept, a parting can sometimes be easier for both the family and the business, causing less stress and less tension. One parent even told us, "I sometimes feel it would be less painful for me if my child were dead. At least then I'd have some closure to our estrangement."

We don't choose our parents, siblings, children, cousins, nieces, nephews, aunts, or uncles. To think that simply because we're born into the same family means we're going to automatically have great relationships and communicate effectively is naïve. It requires skill. It requires desire, knowledge, effort, and practice, and even then it doesn't always work. Changing ineffective communication patterns is tough and requires breaking the mold on how it has been handled in the past. Challenging the status quo can be complex with deep roots, and we're quick to refer clients to a clinician when warranted.

While we typically think of communication as speaking or transmitting a message to others, the other half of communication is all too often overlooked. It's called "listening." The problem with listening is speaking; we're too focused on our own point of view and put too much energy into crafting a response to what the other person is saying, rather than really hearing what is being said. The greatest leaders are listeners, yet how much effort do we put into honing that skill? We're seldom, if ever, taught listening skills in school. Remember the simple yet powerful message of Stephen Covey, "Seek first to understand then to be understood."

TOXIC COMMUNICATION STYLES IN FAMILIES WRECK BUSINESS AND FAMILY RELATIONSHIPS

In our experience with business families, the leading inhibitor to effective communication is the failure to recognize that *what* we say is far less important than *how* we say it. It's all about managing the emotion behind the message—tone, volume, pace, eye contact, posture, facial expression, and gestures.

All of this is lost when we communicate via text and email. Emails and texting are best used for simple information sharing and inquiry, never as a substitute for having a sensitive conversation. (See Addendum #13: Email Protocol.)

Although it may be difficult and require more work, communicating face to face is the most productive and effective form of communication. It gives both parties the opportunity to fully understand where the other person is coming from and participate in an active conversation.

THE LOST ART OF LISTENING

We often encounter families that have become so used to fighting and agitated conversations that it becomes their norm, and the idea of changing it is either scary or doesn't even occur to them. In our observations, it's possible to get used to dysfunctional communication in the same way that it's possible to get used to walking with a stone in your shoe—but neither is optimal, and it's far better to take action to fix what's wrong rather than simply learning to live with it.

A fairly classic example of poor communication is the Bengal sisters, who constantly talk over one another. Neither one speaks in complete sentences or ever gets to finish a thought before the other jumps in and speaks over her. When they disagree, frequently in front of other employees, the fur flies. One tries to make her point. The other interrupts and immediately disagrees. The first one cuts her off and repeats her point, speaking louder and faster. The other interrupts and disagrees again, even louder and faster, and so on, until it becomes a yelling match, which they simply label "a conversation."

The disagreements remain unresolved as one or the other gives up and each retreats to her own corner.

Having seen them in action, we suggested that they practice having their "conversations" in private rather than in front of others. We shared our simple model of effective communication (see Addendum #14: Model of Effective Communication) and helped the sisters practice validating one another before responding. We explained that validating doesn't mean you agree with the other person. Rather, it's a verification that you have heard and understood what the other is saying; it's a powerful expression of respect. Slowly, with much practice and role-playing, they learned to repeat what they heard the other say and actually started to hear one another. One sister once even admitted she was wrong and apologized to the other for the very first time.

The Centaro family serves as a prime example of another type of ineffective communication. Mom built the business from the ground up and brought her two sons in when they were in their twenties. Mom was a bit of a control freak and had a difficult time opening her mind to the ideas of others, hence communicating with her was challenging for her sons. On top of that, one son felt he was far more capable of running the business than his brother, whose head really wasn't in the game. He would show up late and leave early, the classic story we see all too often.

Fast-forward fifteen years, with both sons still in the business and Mom starting to think about slowing down. She made the unilateral decision to promote the more capable son to president, while basically gifting her other son with a title, VP of operations, because she felt guilty that she was only promoting his brother. Because this was never discussed and the expectations around their roles were never managed, conflict ensued, and the brothers became increasingly at odds with each other. Plus, Mom had a controlling mentality and her "mom" preference was lectures vs. conversations; one brother requested that she talk *with* him, not *to* him or *at* him. She was caught in the middle of the dynamic, unable to remove her "mom hat" and address her sons as employees.

Each son would complain to Mom about the other and never speak directly to one another, catching Mom in the middle, resulting in tremendous triangulation among the three of them. This prevented the brothers from addressing the challenges directly with each other, and offered no means of resolution. On top of that, there was classic poor communication, using emails to avoid direct discussions.

We were brought in at the height of the issues, and our first objective was to help them change the way they communicated. One step was to help them realize that so long as Mom continued to be caught in the middle, the brothers would not have any impetus to work toward finding better ways to communicate with each other and thus wouldn't develop conflict resolution skills and the ability to build alignment or manage expectations for the future of the business. Years of dysfunctional communication can't be resolved overnight, but with feedback and support and the sincere efforts made by all to change their style, meaningful progress has been made.

The Riley family is a fourth-generation manufacturing business that recently transitioned the ownership and leadership to the next generation of three siblings: two sons and a daughter. The oldest son was the leadership heir apparent and excellent at managing the operations of the business, while the other two focused on sales and marketing and never appreciated the complexity of running the business as a whole. Stuck in their silos, the three siblings would argue over decisions in the business, with no real means of effectively cooperating with each other to resolve their differences and make major decisions. Whenever they would get together, they would bicker, talk over each other, and dwell on past conflicts and injuries, while accomplishing little to nothing thanks to their inadequate communication skills. As in the Centaro family, they also depended to an unhealthy extent on email and texts to deliver messages they weren't comfortable giving each other face-to-face.

CAUTION: EFFECTIVE COMMUNICATION CAN BE HABIT FORMING

We introduced the three siblings to the notion of using a talking stick to control who could speak at any given time in a meeting. We also coached them to let go of the past. In order for the three of them to move on, they needed to address their past issues, accept their differences, and forgive one another. The risk of not forgiving is to be held hostage by the others, thus impeding their ability to move on. Once they were able to focus on the future, as well as feel heard and understood, they were able to build alignment on the strategy of the business, which helped them with effective decision making.

Sadly, not every family communications breakdown can be fixed; underlying issues are so deep, and some people are simply too enmeshed in their dysfunctional ways to change. Referred to us by their attorney, the Jennings family is an example of this dynamic. The father and owner, Jared, felt obligated to call us—on his attorney's suggestion, not from a desire for change. Jared has two sons and a daughter in the business with him. Instantly identifiable was their inability to communicate in any effective way. When the siblings spoke, emailed, or texted, their messages were invariably critical, harsh, and aggressive. One underlying issue was less about the kids and how they communicated with each other and more about how they wanted to communicate with Dad.

The challenge here was that Dad had zero interest in hearing from his children about the business and the changes they wanted to make. Thus, any time his children wanted to bring up issues in the business, he simply shut them down. This was a real dilemma because the three kids had different skills and different visions of what they wanted to do. It wasn't just about following directly in Dad's footsteps and running the business exactly the way he ran it.

Jared's daughter was particularly entrepreneurial, looking for other ways to bring new products and revenue into the business, plus delegating and building a team, versus just grinding away like Dad, who was at the office six days a week. Jared would wave off any attempts to talk about change, to work with his children, or even to refer them to counseling—effectively shutting down further discussion. He really didn't want to give up his leadership role, and keeping the kids at odds with one another accomplished that. When we shared that truth with him, it didn't go over well.

Our brief engagement ended for a few other reasons. First, Dad wasn't genuinely invested in the process from the outset. When one son wanted to assume some responsibility from Dad, he told us Dad acted like he was stealing something from him. Second, Dad blamed his children's ineffective communication and wouldn't accept any culpability himself; and third, he refused to have the difficult conversations directly with his children. Fourth, probably in addition to abundant other underlying reasons, he refused to acknowledge the consequences of his actions. He knew that if we helped improve their communication, create appropriate roles and responsibilities, design better decision-making processes, build a team, and forge alignment for future strategy, then he'd be required to start to think about his future in the company and, frankly, he was terrified he would no longer be relevant. And so, ultimately, we were let go.

Our work requires major commitment on the part of our clients, who must accept us as catalysts for change and be willing make a serious and substantial emotional commitment, time commitment, and financial commitment if progress is to be made. If a client is not willing to commit on all three even when the going gets tough, then the engagement is more likely than not to be unsuccessful. Family members must see the process through; it's sometimes a rocky road and can get more so before it gets better. That's exactly what happened for Jared Jennings; it was painful as we pushed for more candid communication because we were uncovering a wound and cleaning it out, and it stung. That's when Jared started canceling meetings, and the engagement ended prematurely.

The fact is, despite the best resolve in the world, you can't help fix something when somebody won't let you reveal and address the underlying issues. It just can't be done. Fortunately, the vast majority of our client families enjoy real success through the process.

PAUL'S PERSPECTIVE

Early in business in staff meetings, feeling bright eyed and bushy tailed (ever the young bull), I was eager to share how much I knew. It took me a while, but I learned that if I slowed down, listened better, asked questions, held off speaking, and gained alliance by building on the points of others, my comments would be better received.

The greatest challenge I had with my dad was the differences in our communication styles. My dad's speaking style tended to be inductive, gradually working up to the point he wanted to make. My listening preference is deductive; I need the bottom line first. Wearing my hat as a son, I don't recall being frustrated by this, because he wasn't prone to long explanations, yet in business it was a hindrance until I could understand our differences and gain patience and the ability to endure what, at times, seemed like a conversation going nowhere. I learned to grant my dad the benefit of the doubt and realize he was making a point preceded by abundant information that seemed irrelevant until I listened to the end.

Another communication issue with my dad was around respect for time. Our offices were connected to one another through a backdoor and, early on, with an ever-high sense of urgency, I'd come through many times a day with a question or something I wanted to share with him. It didn't occur to me that I was interrupting whatever he was doing with my relatively unimportant matters until my dad presented me with a pad of purple lined paper. He suggested I make notes on whatever I wanted to talk to him about and, if the matters were not urgent, to hold off on sharing them until our daily luncheons. Another lesson learned.

DAVID'S PERSPECTIVE

Healthy communication requires respect for boundaries. When my dad and I started our business, I had been working from home with another company, and I had a second phone line just for business. We decided to stick with that arrangement to create healthy boundaries around our communication with respect to our families. My father will call me or I'll call him on our dedicated business line, and we'll talk for hours about a client or new business objective. Then we'll hang up, and two minutes later he'll call on the house line. I'll pick up, and he'll say, "Can I talk to Adam?"—or Lily or Jenny or me—but it has nothing to do with business. It's strictly about our family life. It's about managing expectations, so I know when the phone rings on my business line and it's Dad, then we're talking about business. But if he calls on the personal line, the expectation is that it's about family.

Boundaries also extend to time we spend together. We're scrupulous about not talking business at family events, whether that's July 4th weekend or Labor Day weekend, both of which we typically spend with our extended family. That wouldn't be fair to us, because it's time for us to be with our family, and it wouldn't be fair to the rest of our family, because business talk can be exclusionary.

I'm also quite conscious of the best time of day to communicate with my father. If I need to speak with him about something important, I generally do it in the morning because I know that's when he's at his best and most focused. It's not fair to him, or to me, to try to have an in-depth discussion late in the afternoon, since I know he's been up since four or five in the morning. I often tell that story to our clients, as an example of how to pick the right time to talk to somebody. My dad also knows if I'm hungry or hot, it's probably not the best time to talk to me. It sounds crazy—but you have to understand the mind-set of the other person and plan thoughtfully about the optimal times to have substantive conversations.

I remind my dad of the purple pad of paper my grandfather gave him because his sense of urgency has not diminished in seventy years—so if he has several topics to talk to me about, do me a favor, bulk it in an email, and send it to me. But please don't blast ten emails on ten different thoughts. It just clutters my inbox, and I ultimately won't get to it. He understands that and is considerate about it (most of the time).

One evening, my dad wanted to speak with me about an important matter that involved a meeting on the following day, so he sent me a crisp email with nothing in the subject field, and in the body of the message simply typed, "Call me." When I read the email, I interpreted Dad's message as anger or that something was wrong, and for a while I pondered what I might have done to make him upset with me. When I called, I asked if he was angry with me, and my father replied, "No, not at all," and he explained that the brevity, perceived by me as being curt, was simply because he was tired but didn't want to initiate the call, wanting to respect my family time. Fortunately, we have the kind of relationship that allows this type of dialogue.

Imagine how easy it would've been to misinterpret a simple act without questioning it further, without "seeking first to understand," and how I might have reacted to him the following day had it not been clarified. And this is a really important point: many of our clients jump to assumptions or conclusions based on the limited information they have, and it's generally inaccurate. People are compelled to finish stories in their minds with whatever information they have. Whether they have all of it or they have little of it, we as humans are compelled to draw conclusions. The problem is, when we have limited information, the conclusions we form are often inaccurate. I saw that in my interaction with my father and learned not to make those assumptions again. At the same time, the lesson he learned was if he wants me to call him, he ought to say, "Hey, I just want to chat with you about something. Everything's fine—when you get a second, give me a call." And since we had that conversation, it's never happened again.

Because of our profession and what we do, we live our lives on what we call "a meta-level" where we respectfully question and reflect on how we communicate with each other. We really work to be clear on where each of us is coming from. We work hard at not jumping to conclusions, to the extent that we sometimes *hyper*communicate— but, with communication, better too much than too little.

Our partnership works because we have a solid foundation in our relationship with one another of candor and trust, openness and respect. Those life values are part of our culture. It doesn't mean we agree on everything; that's not possible. But we do know how to disagree and not be disagreeable. Conflict is inevitable; the difference between successful and unsuccessful family businesses is how you manage the conflict.

GUIDELINES FOR SUSTAINABILITY

- Relearn communication styles that are culturally engrained.

- Remember the words of Stephen Covey, "Seek first to understand then to be understood."

- Communicate by listening more and speaking less. We have two ears and one mouth, and we need to use them proportionately.

- Avoid triangulation.

- Hold difficult conversations face-to-face, not by email or text.

- Recognize the impact of nonverbal communication

- Be patient: learning good communication practices takes time.

- Avoid interrupting and talking over one another.

- Find the underlying need for "hyperinfomating."

- Be transparent to foster good communication.

- Be willing to endure it; candid communication can be painful.

- Build alliances on the remarks of others; it can often help others hear you better.

- Heighten your self-awareness.

- Understand the listening and speaking preferences of others (as well as your own). Use the speaking style, inductive or deductive, most likely to connect with the listener. (See Addendum #15: Inductive vs. Deductive Communication Styles, by Dr. Ethan Becker.)

- Have respect for time and other boundaries.

- Be careful of cryptic messages.

SOME FURTHER COMMUNICATION TIPS

- Remember that emotion trumps reason, and we're seldom aware of it when communicating with other people.

- Do your best to manage your emotions when trying to have difficult conversations. "Manage" doesn't mean quell, it means control; be in charge of your emotions, and sometimes that means expressing how you *feel* before expressing what you *think.*

- Our biggest listening failure occurs because too much of our energy is spent crafting a response to what's being said while it's being said. Here are some listening suggestions:

    □ Focus.

    □ Quell your own thoughts.

    □ Maintain eye contact.

    □ Listen to tone, volume, and pace.

    □ Watch body language and facial expressions.

    □ Hear what is not said.

- □ Stop assuming you've heard it all before.

- □ Resist defensiveness and stay open minded.

- Validate others. When people don't feel they have been heard or validated, they won't hear you. This is where conversations escalate and get louder.

- Consider the timing relative to the situation and time of day (and whether the other person is hot, tired, or hungry).

- Select an appropriate, perhaps private, location.

- Ask clarifying questions.

- Address the issue, versus reacting to the issue.

- Grant forgiveness. Like validation, forgiveness doesn't mean you agree. It means you are letting it go and moving on. It takes time, but failure to do so lets the other person hold you hostage.

- Take a risk: Make yourself vulnerable. Admit when you're wrong. Apologizing can be a very powerful tool, but you must own the apology with no "buts" after it.

- In group settings, seek an alliance. Be the last one to talk, and build on the thoughts of others.

- Consider a code of conduct (see chapter 7).

- Compromise, but don't compromise yourself.

- Be willing to address tough issues. As our friend, Sam Lorusso Jr., says, "Difficult conversations with people are even more difficult when you only have them with yourself."

In Conclusion...

■ ▨ ■

Our business byline is "Catalyst for Change." Our mission is to help family members in business together enjoy Thanksgiving dinner with one another.

In many instances, we serve as referees. Early on, in a meeting with a family business and helping to resolve an issue, the mom said we should wear stripes (like a referee). We thought that was a great idea. Ever since, in meeting with client families, we wear stripes.

Without referees, there would be mayhem; imagine football or hockey without referees! They keep the rules of the game intact, they keep control of the situation, and they keep the environment safe. Much like referees in sports, our job is to create a safe environment to allow clients to do difficult work. In a safe environment, they can open up. They can be candid, they can be transparent, and they can be honest with each other, knowing that we're there to support them and to manage whatever challenges might ensue.

In addition, we wear stripes because it sets the expectation of the engagement; we are the facilitators, so our clients can be the participants. This frees them to be active contributors and allows us to manage the dynamics of the meeting, the agenda, the situation, the notes—everything. It allows them to strictly focus on doing the work we're there to do with them.

Seeing us in stripes helps our clients get into the right mind-set to address the difficult issues they must tackle with other family members. We explain that to them ahead of time. And on the day we show up to a meeting in shirts that aren't striped and hand our clients a baton (see Addendum #16: Baton), the clients know, in our estimation, they're over the hump.

We've worked with businesses with fewer than a dozen employees to businesses with thousands of employees and with businesses with revenues from a million dollars to a billion dollars. It's not the number of zeros at the end of the number that makes the difference. It's the nature and complexity of relationships among the family members that makes the difference.

This book covers just a minute portion of the more common themes from our experiences with the thousands of business families we've either met, consulted with, or whose stories we've heard. It's an infinitesimal part of the topic as a whole. There's so much we continue to learn and experience. We invite you to visit our website at FamBizConsulting.com, where you'll find hundreds of links to useful articles, videos, and other information. We welcome you to connect with us—to share your story, to ask a question, or to simply offer a thought or comment.

We can be reached at info@FamBizConsulting.com.

PAUL KAROFSKY AND DAVID KAROFSKY

Addenda

■ ▩ ■

#1 Boston Sunday Herald

#2 300 Summer Street

#3 Etched Stock Certificate

#4 Job Description and Percent of Time Chart

#5 Responsibility Charting

#6 The Key

#7 Old TCG Logo

#8 Max's Family Code of Conduct

#9 The Horizontal Bar

#10 The Multi-Roles Model

#11 Common Role of Family
Business Board of Directors

#12 The Attributes of Leadership Checklist©

#13 Email Protocol

#14 Model of Effective Communication

#15 Inductive vs. Deductive Communication Styles

#16 The Baton

#17 Family Business Health Check

#18 The Man in the Glass

#19 Family Business Transition

#1: BOSTON SUNDAY HERALD

This is the front page of the Boston Sunday Herald from March 1, 1959 and the article that details the loss of our family's wallcovering distribution center.

#2: 300 SUMMER STREET

This is the building at 300 Summer Street in Boston to which we moved (and ultimately purchased) after the fire in Roxbury.

#3: ETCHED STOCK CERTIFICATE

This is the stock certificate of the newly incorporated business, etched on glass, which Paul gave David.

#4: JOB DESCRIPTION AND % OF TIME CHART

TRANSITION CONSULTING GROUP
CATALYSTS FOR CHANGE IN FAMILY BUSINESS

Date:
Name:
Title:
Position summary:

Primary responsibilities/essential tasks:

__% = the average percentage of working time expected to be spent on each responsibility

   • = the essential tasks for which the incumbent is responsible

__% •

__% •

__% •

__% •

__% •

__% •

__% •

Personal attributes:

Reporting relationships (titles/job functions of people reporting to you):

#5: RESPONSIBILITY CHARTING

TRANSITION CONSULTING GROUP
CATALYSTS FOR CHANGE IN FAMILY BUSINESS

ROLES:

R = the one individual responsible for the role/task (can be only one person)

A/V = holds the power of final approval or veto (can be multiple people)

S = a support role: provides assistance only as and when requested to do so (can be multiple people)

I = kept informed (by R) as to progress of the project and detailed tasks (can be multiple people)

Champion = the coordinator/facilitator of the broad initiative

Initiative = the broad action step, whereas the "task" is the detailed action to be taken

INITIATIVE: **DATE:**   **CHAMPION:**

TASK	DATE	R	A/V	S	I

#6: THE KEY

This is the key Paul's father mounted on green velvet and returned to him after he completed the OPM Program.

The plaque reads:

"More important than knowledge, is the key to imagination. It can open hearts, minds, doors and even pocketbooks." It was signed, "FUF."

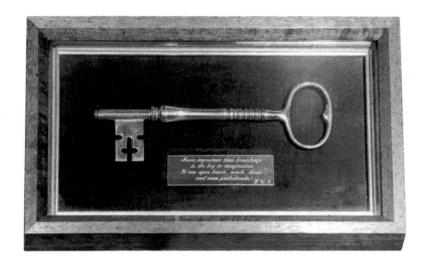

#7: OLD TCG LOGO

This is the original Transition Consulting Group logo. The swirls are an adaptation of the Taguiri-Davis 3-Circle Model. In this shaded form they represent the continuous movement and change in family business relationships and dynamics. David urged the change to a simpler logo, more suitable for electronic use.

#8: MAX'S FAMILY CODE OF CONDUCT

- We will treat each other with care, compassion, and respect.
- We will give each other frequent positive reinforcement.
- We will have quarterly family business meetings.
- We will make time for each other one of our own priorities.
- We will offer suggestions to each other rather than complaints.
- We will work on our listening skills and try not to talk over one another.
- We will keep positive comments positive, with no "buts" or negative additions.
- We recognize that it is often difficult to talk about feelings, but we agree to speak directly to each other about our feelings and needs, listen with full attention, and maintain eye contact.
- We will freely apologize and not leave each other in anger.
- If answers to our questions are too vague, it is okay to ask for expansion or clarification.
- We will accept that some questions may not be answerable.
- We will spend some family time together. This will be "play/ recreational time" with no discussion of business.
- We will use humor freely and avoid sarcasm.
- We recognize that this Code of Conduct is a "work in progress" and will review it periodically. We will respect it and add to it in writing as appropriate.
- We will call infractions to one another's attention immediately and respectfully.
- We will be accountable to each other.

#9: THE HORIZONTAL BAR

TRANSITION CONSULTING GROUP
CATALYSTS FOR CHANGE IN FAMILY BUSINESS

The horizontal bar is the mindset which we encourage family stakeholders to adopt when they are in a planning mode, lest they get caught up and consumed by their silos. Failure to do so, limits creative thinking and responsiveness to others.

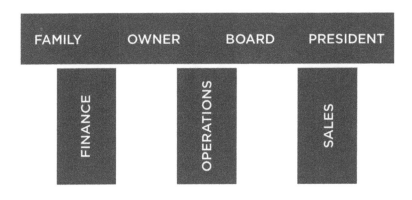

#10: THE MULTI-ROLES MODEL

Roles of Family, Ownership, Governance, and Management

Since the 1980s, the Taguiri-Davis 3 Circle Model© has been the hallmark graphic of family business. In its exquisite simplicity, it allows for an understanding of the differing roles and interrelationships of family members, owners, and those who work in the business. Some have adapted the model, combining governance with ownership. The research and writings of John Ward and Randel Carlock, among others, have given increased attention to governance matters. Their work, and the preponderance of independent directors on business family boards, suggests that a model which adds **governance** as a *fourth system,* might help us understand the differing perspectives of the resulting fifteen (vs. seven) subsystems. The Multi-Roles Model© is an attempt to do that.

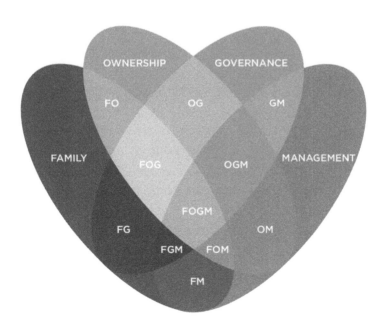

Differing Perspectives in the Multi-Roles Model©

1. **Family (F)** = family members who have no role in ownership, governance, or management. Examples may include spouses, in-laws, young children, or adult family members who may have grown up in a business family and/or feel a sense of attachment to a business owned by their spouses, siblings, parents, or children. Typical interests and concerns: family first, history, culture, values, fairness, equality, and inclusion. Positioning often includes "fighting for the spouse who works in the business." For others, there may be feelings of disinterest in the business.

2. **Ownership (O)** = owners who are not family members, not involved in governance, and not managers in the company. Examples may include shareholders in publicly held family businesses or silent partners, limited partners, or other investors. Typical interests and concerns: "strictly" business performance; rising stock price, profitability, and dividends; often focused on short-term results; want of a professionally managed business free from interference by family issues and battles for control.

3. **Governance (G)** = people who have a governance role and are neither family members, owners, nor managers. These "outside" directors are ideally "neutral and objective watch dogs" though often allied with one or more family member shareholders. Typical interests and concerns: the "big" picture, representing the shareholders as a group, increasing shareholder value, performance of key executives, strategy, sustainability, meeting potentially diverse shareholder needs not at the expense of the business.

4. **Management (M)** = managers (or other employees) who are not family members, have no ownership stake, and do not have a role in governance. Typical interests and concerns: day-to-day operations, short-term issues, preserving/

enhancing their own position in the organization (i.e., job security and career tracking), autonomy.

5. **FO** = family members who are owners but are neither managers nor have a role in governance. Examples often include children who have been gifted stock for tax planning purposes or have inherited shares for reasons of "fairness." Typical interests and concerns: cash distributions, fairness of employed family members' compensation and perks, liquidity, employment for self, community perceptions. Some have a keen sense of stewardship and wish to preserve the business for the next generation. Others are self-focused, asking, "How can I benefit from this business?" Some are ambivalent about ownership and desirous of exit options. They are often in conflict with FOGs.

6. **FG** = family members who have a role in governance but are neither owners nor managers. Examples may include members of the senior generation who have transitioned ownership and leadership to the next generation. Typical interests and concerns: how business "was," what they could or couldn't do, how next generation will "measure up," possibly their having "let go" too soon. Others are cultural icons and still retain significant informal control and play a major role perpetuating values and guiding the next generation of leaders. Some are spouses of FOGMs to ensure board control.

7. **FM** = family members who are managers (or employees) in the company but have neither an ownership stake nor a role in governance. Examples often include siblings or cousins of entrepreneurs or children who have not yet been granted an ownership stake. Typical concerns and interests: their own role and responsibility, their future security, fairness, acquiring an ownership stake. They are often in conflict with FOMs.

8. **OG** = nonfamily owners who have a governance role but are not involved in management. Examples may include investors with seats on the board or representatives of venture capital firms. They are often focused on more immediate returns, distributions, and a three-to-five-year exit/M&A strategy for the business. They are often in conflict with family members.

9. **OM** = nonfamily member managers who are owners with no governance role. Examples often include nonfamily employees who have been granted stock in companies where the family typically retains the governance role or where there are many such employees in an equity position, such as in an ESOP. Many are in a publicly owned family business. Interests include job security, dividends, and stock growth.

10. **GM** = nonfamily member managers who are involved in governance yet have no ownership stake. Examples often include professional "C" level key nonfamily executives like the chief financial officer or nonfamily president or CEO. Roles often include mentoring the younger generation and helping to address family differences. They often wish to be OGMs.

11. **FOG** = family member owners who have a governance role but are not in management. Examples often include former FOGMs. Others may be family members with a different career who have inherited a significant ownership stake or spouses who are inactive in the business and have token board roles. Some who are focused on stewardship and long-term wealth creation may be in conflict with others who are more focused on immediate or short-term rewards. Some need help to clarify boundaries with Ms.

12. **FOM** = family member owners who are managers but are not involved in governance. Examples are common in third generation or older family businesses or in situations where a large number of family members are owner-managers.

Role is often accompanied by frustration about not having a governance role.

13. **FGM** = non-owner family member managers who are involved in governance. Examples may include seniors who have divested their equity or in-laws who have other businesses and have a role in governance in a business in which their spouses have an ownership stake. Others may include cousins or spouses who work in the company and have a token governance role.

14. **OGM** = nonfamily member managers with an ownership stake and a role in governance. Examples often include key nonfamily managers who have been granted or purchased an equity position. Their role is often to help keep family members under control and family issues out of the boardroom.

15. **FOGM** = family member owners who are managers and involved in governance. Examples typically include "C" level family member leaders and emerging leaders in the enterprise.

#11: COMMON ROLE OF FAMILY BUSINESS BOARD OF DIRECTORS

TRANSITION CONSULTING GROUP
Catalysts for Change in Family Business

COMMON ROLE OF FAMILY BUSINESS BOARD OF DIRECTORS

- to consider, protect, and represent the interests and goals of the shareholders
- to appoint the CEO and oversee his/her performance
- to establish CEO compensation
- to review corporate objectives
- to approve major acquisitions, divestitures, capital expenditures, and operating budgets
- to advise the CEO and the senior management team
- to approve debt/equity ratios and lending activity
- to assure that dividend policy effectively balances the needs of the family and the business
- to consider major organizational restructuring
- to guide and assure contingency and succession planning
- to provide skills and expertise for seeing the big picture
- to evaluate its own performance
- to formulate and evaluate long-term strategic plans
- to help mentor the younger generation

#12: THE ATTRIBUTES OF LEADERSHIP CHECKLIST©

TRANSITION CONSULTING GROUP
CATALYSTS FOR CHANGE IN FAMILY BUSINESS

THE ATTRIBUTES OF LEADERSHIP CHECKLIST©

How do leaders lead? What do they do?
What attributes do they possess?

How well do these attributes apply to you and
other current or emerging leaders?

(Adapted in part and inspired by Harry Levinson's "Criteria for choosing chief executives," *Harvard Business Review*. No. 80410; John Ward and Craig Aronoff, Nation's Business, April, 1994, p. 54; Another Kind of Hero; and Tom Peters' *The Pursuit of Wow!*, p. 279-281.)

A. Conceptual capacity

1. _____ is a strategic problem solver.

2. _____ sees the whole picture and its implications.

3. _____ thinks both short and long term.

4. _____ distills, abstracts, conceptualizes, focuses, organizes, and integrates information.

5. _____ learns from experience; has good street smarts.

6. _____ is intelligent; is both abstract and practical.

7. _____ has sound judgment; knows when to act.

8. _____ seeks expanding horizons; has vision.

9. _____ has a presence.

10. _____ receives information readily; blends multiple opinions into consensus.

11. _____ is imaginative and creative.

B. Capacity to understand and manage ones' self and others

1. _____ tolerates ambiguity and confusion.

2. _____ can multitask.

3. _____ is enthusiastic; genuinely loves the job.

4. _____ is committed to lifelong education and training for self and others.

5. _____ is able to endure loneliness; works with minimal feedback from higher up.

6. _____ has finger on pulse of the organization, its stake-holders, and competitors.

7. _____ paces self well.

8. _____ competently manages stress.

9. _____ has appropriate sense of humor.

10. _____ has appropriate sense of urgency.

11. _____ uses time effectively; is a vigorous planner; is very well organized.

12. _____ is credible and ethical; has sound integrity.

13. _____ recognizes and acts on social responsibility.

14. _____ understands self and assesses self honestly.

15. _____ is emotionally strong, yet unpretentious; is willing to admit mistakes.

16. _____ makes use of a personal counselor and confidant.

17. _____ is politically sensitive.

18. _____ supports a mechanism for resolving family conflict.

19. _____ supports objective assessment of family members' knowledge, skill, and experience.

20. _____ recognizes issues of family rivalry and seeks facilitation when appropriate

21. _____ recognizes the difficulty of the senior generation "letting go."

C. Capacity to "take charge" and act

1. _____ is authoritative; takes charge.

2. _____ demands performance from others.

3. _____ expresses convictions confidently; is a "straight shooter."

4. _____ is accessible; is supportive in times of personal and business need or crisis.

5. _____ shares power; delegates effectively and defines accountability.

6. _____ has consistently high energy level.

7. _____ inspires and guides others.

8. _____ communicates effectively; is an especially good listener.

9. _____ builds and sustains culture.

10. _____ is motivated to achieve for the organization's sake.

11. _____ has a passion for excellence.

12. _____ sets clear goals consistent with the purpose, needs, and values of the organization.

13. _____ manages conflict effectively.

14. _____ is sensitive, perceptive, and insightful.

15. _____ believes in the capacity of people to grow; is able to develop others for sustainability.

16. _____ likes, respects, and relates well to a diverse population.

17. _____ cares for others with warmth; is empathic.

18. _____ stands on own but welcomes information, advice, criticism, and cooperation from others.

19. _____ is involved, participative, and interdependent.

20. _____ copes effectively; readily adapts.

21. _____ is even-tempered.

22. _____ has little tolerance for obstacles, circumvents them; is optimistic and solution focused.

23. _____ assumes accountability.

24. _____ has little tolerance for procrastination and bureaucracy.

25. _____ anticipates, advocates, and facilitates change; overcomes resistance to change.

26. _____ is willing to experiment and take risks; readily exits comfort zone.

27. _____ is consistent in thinking and behavior.

#13: EMAIL PROTOCOL

TRANSITION CONSULTING GROUP
CATALYSTS FOR CHANGE IN FAMILY BUSINESS

When and How to Best Use E-Mail

Most of the articles on the web about the inappropriate use of e-mails refer to security, personal use issues, and sharing offensive material in the workplace. In our work with family and closely held businesses, we know that their concerns are far more reaching. They center on "courtesy" vs. "rudeness" or downright "hostility." So here are some suggested "dos" and "don'ts" around e-mail usage.

1. Resist using e-mail when a phone call might be better.

2. Keep the "subject" line brief.

3. Keep the formatting simple.

4. Have a courteous greeting and closing.

5. Be concise. Make it easy for the reader to grasp the content quickly. Break your message into paragraphs if appropriate, and use "headers."

6. Abrupt or cryptic messages are easily misinterpreted. Consider writing in full sentences.

7. Neither tone, nor volume, nor inflections, nor body language are available to the reader. Be aware how they might be interpreted from your choice of words.

8. Sarcasm is exceedingly dangerous.

9. The reader may read your e-mail more than once. Consider how your message might be interpreted when re-read at a later date.

10. It's easy to hide behind the screen and send rude e-mails when you are angry. Be polite.

11. If you receive a hostile e-mail (in e-mail lingo called a "flame-a-gram"), resist replying immediately, if at all. Think about addressing the e-mail, not responding to the e-mail.

12. If you must reply to a hostile e-mail, wait at least twenty-four hours to do so.

13. Don't hide behind e-mail. Ask yourself if you would say the same thing face-to-face.

14. Be careful with the use of CAPITAL LETTERS. They are typically interpreted as SHOUTING.

15. Your e-mail may be forwarded to others. Be sure this is how you wish to be perceived.

16. Caution when using the cc: field. Many people do not wish to have their e-mail addresses passed around with a lot of others whom they may not know well (or at all). It can also be perceived that you are cc-ing someone to throw the recipient under the bus (like cc-ing his or her boss).

17. Only reply to those who need to see your reply.

18. Reply in a timely manner. We tend to assume that our e-mails are read by others within a minute of our sending them. Then, of course, we expect an instant reply. When we don't get one, we assume the recipient is ignoring us, and then we wonder why. If you need a quick reply, let the person know that when you send the e-mail.

19. Use the return receipt only when it is critical to know when the e-mail is opened.

20. When forwarding e-mails, be sure to delete other e-mail addresses and commentary from other forwarders.

21. Use spell-check for possible spelling and grammar errors. Spelling errors are perceived as sloppiness, laziness, or lack of education.

22. Establish a company policy on e-mail use. Specifically address personal use, abusive or offensive material, policy on receiving offensive material from other employees, etc.

23. Use appropriate signoff. If replying, you may wish to mirror the signoff of the sender. Some gurus suggest that "sincerely" is always safe. Same with "yours truly" and "regards"; reserve "best" for those whom you know well.

24. Don't keep "thank you" as a permanent part of your signoff. Sometimes it may not apply.

25. Your e-mails are a reflection of yourself—your personality and style. Re-read e-mails before sending them with this in mind: "Is this how I want to be perceived by the recipient?"

26. Resist bombarding people with single thoughts or questions e-mail after e-mail. It might make more sense to save an e-mail in drafts and simply add thoughts/questions to it as the day goes along and then send it at a later time.

Texting is different: Though shortcuts, incomplete sentences, and abbreviations abound, we still encourage caution on how "tone" is perceived. It's also an inappropriate medium for negative feedback.

#14: MODEL OF EFFECTIVE COMMUNICATION

TRANSITION CONSULTING GROUP
CATALYSTS FOR CHANGE IN FAMILY BUSINESS

MODEL OF EFFECTIVE COMMUNICATION

All too often, in difficult conversations, when an issue is raised, there's some brief back and forth discussion. The conversation gets heated, frustration is evidenced and emotions take over. Often dialogue gets louder and louder as people react to one another or one party backs off and the discussion ends with no resolution.

We encourage a model where we validate what the other has said, by acknowledging and restating his/her words. This doesn't mean we agree, it means we understand where the other is coming from. And if we don't understand, it's appropriate to ask questions to clarify, then validate. This can dilute the emotion and allow for a rational response, rather than an emotional reaction.

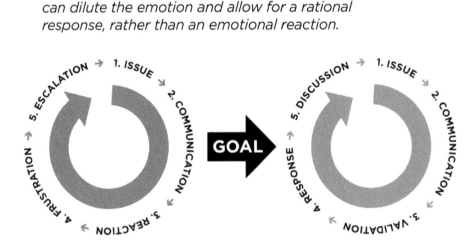

1. ISSUE	1. ISSUE
2. COMMUNICATION	2. COMMUNICATION
3. REACTION	3. VALIDATION
4. FRUSTRATION	4. RESPONSE
5. ESCALATION	5. DISCUSSION

#15: INDUCTIVE VS. DEDUCTIVE COMMUNICATION STYLES

TRANSITION CONSULTING GROUP
CATALYSTS FOR CHANGE IN FAMILY BUSINESS

Adapted with permission from Dr. Ethan Becker, the Speech Improvement Company.

We refer you to The Speech Improvement Company, (speechimprovemement.com) and Dr. Becker's book, Mastering Communication at Work: How to Lead, Manage and Influence.

INDUCTIVE	DEDUCTIVE
Supporting point	Main point
Supporting point	Supporting point
Supporting point	Supporting point
Main point	Supporting point

#16: THE BATON

This is Transition Consulting Group's baton. David has one, knowing that the mantle of TCG's leadership has been firmly passed to him. As our clients and members of The Peer Alliance reach similar levels of leadership autonomy, they are presented with one as well.

#17: FAMILY BUSINESS HEALTH CHECK

This is an abbreviated version of our "Family Business Health Check(c)." Go to fambizconsulting.com for the full version. It allows for some self-reflection and feedback on how your family enterprise is doing.

FAMILY BUSINESS
HEALTH
CHECK

How healthy is your family business?
Successful family enterprises demonstrate healthy business behavior from creating clear roles & responsibilities and decision making processes to implementing work/life boundaries and strategic planning.

The following questions are designed to spark your curiosity as to the health of your family enterprise. All of your answers are kept completely confidential.

BACKGROUND INFORMATION

Name_____

Company_____

Email_____ Phone_____

What generation is your family business? _____ How many family members are in your family business? _____

How many employees do you have in your family business? _____

FAMILY BUSINESS HEALTH QUESTIONS

(Please select the extent to which you agree with the statements below)

	COMPLETELY DISAGREE	MOSTLY DISAGREE	SOMEWHAT AGREE	AGREE	MOSTLY AGREE	COMPLETELY AGREE
We have clear entry and exit criteria for family members.	☐	☐	☐	☐	☐	☐
We have a clear understanding of our roles and responsibilities.	☐	☐	☐	☐	☐	☐
The quality of communication among family members is good.	☐	☐	☐	☐	☐	☐
We have a clear decision making process.	☐	☐	☐	☐	☐	☐
We meet regularly as a family.	☐	☐	☐	☐	☐	☐
We share a vision for the future of the business.	☐	☐	☐	☐	☐	☐
We are aligned on business strategy.	☐	☐	☐	☐	☐	☐
The future of leadership is clear.	☐	☐	☐	☐	☐	☐
The senior generation is ready to "let go."	☐	☐	☐	☐	☐	☐
The future of ownership is clear.	☐	☐	☐	☐	☐	☐

TRANSITION CONSULTING GROUP
CATALYSTS FOR CHANGE IN FAMILY BUSINESS

Framingham, MA | 508.875.7751 | info@FamBizConsulting.com | www.FamBizConsulting.com

#18: THE MAN IN THE GLASS

When you get what you want in your struggle for self
And the world makes you king for a day
Just go to the mirror and look at yourself
And see what that man has to say.

For it isn't your father, or mother, or wife
Whose judgment upon you must pass
The fellow whose verdict counts most in your life
Is the one staring back from the glass.

He's the fellow to please—never mind all the rest
For he's with you, clear to the end
And you've passed your most difficult, dangerous test
If the man in the glass is your friend.

You may fool the whole world down the pathway of years
And get pats on the back as you pass
But your final reward will be heartache and tears
If you've cheated the man in the glass.

By Peter Dale Wimbrow Sr. © 1934

#19: FAMILY BUSINESS TRANSITION

Illustration from David's presentation at a conference for business families in April, 2015.

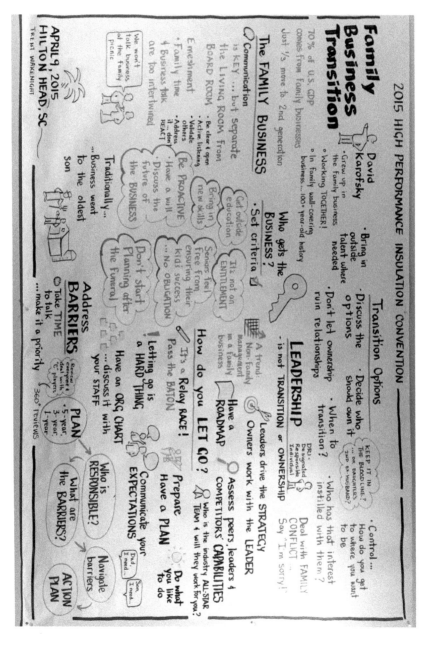

About the Authors

■ ■ ■

PAUL KAROFSKY

After twenty-two years, mostly as a third-generation CEO in his family's distribution business, Paul Karofsky sold the company and earned his EdM from Harvard University, focused on the psychosocial lives of families and intergenerational relationships. He is executive director emeritus of Northeastern University's Center for Family Business, which he helped launch and where he created and facilitated the center's Leadership Development Forum, which was endowed and named in his honor. Paul is a former member of the board of directors of the Family Firm Institute and holds a Certificate in Family Business Advising with Fellow Status. He is a recipient of the institute's Hollander Award and a member of the faculty of FFI's Global Education Network. Also trained as a mediator, Paul was a columnist for *Family Office Review*, a peer reviewer for Harvard University Press, a monthly columnist for *BusinessWeek Online*, and a case study editor of *Nation's Business* and *Families in Business*. Married for fifty years, he and his wife have two spectacular children and four scrumptious grandchildren. He is a member of WPO/YPO, where he was acclaimed "an outstanding resource." Paul is founder of Transition Consulting Group. He serves, internationally, as a consultant to families, businesses, and educational institutions.

He can be reached at Paul@FamBizConsulting.com.

About the Authors

■ ▪ ■

DAVID KAROFSKY

David Karofsky has over twenty-five years of experience coaching and consulting to individuals, families, and businesses to develop better cross-team communication and build alignment among the senior management team. His client work is focused on executing the transition of ownership and leadership, professional development, conflict resolution, strategic planning, and forming governance structures for family and closely held businesses. Prior to partnering with his father at Transition Consulting Group, David spent ten years in hi-tech, holding corporate roles including managing operations for worldwide marketing for a Fortune 100 company and vice president of marketing for a software start-up where he helped launch the company and raise VC funding. David is a graduate of Bowdoin College and received his EdM in counseling psychology from Boston University and his MBA from Northeastern University, where he was awarded a full academic scholarship while working as a teaching assistant for undergraduate business courses. The recipient of multiple achievement awards, David has been a guest speaker internationally and serves on the Marketing Career Track Advisory Board at Northeastern University's Graduate School of Business. He is a founding member and former chair of the Boston chapter of the Young Presidents' Organization's Young Adult Forum and a member of the Family Firm Institute.

David can be reached at David@FamBizConsulting.com.

*Want to explore the challenges
and opportunities in your family business?*

■ ▨ ■

TRANSITION CONSULTING GROUP
CATALYSTS FOR CHANGE IN FAMILY BUSINESS

Transition Consulting Group would be pleased to talk with you to explore the challenges and opportunities facing your family's business.

In working with hundreds of families and their business interests, there's very little we haven't seen. The range of concerns is broad—from communication to conflict resolution, entry to exit, through leadership development and strategies from succession to acquisitions and divestitures. Your family enterprise will benefit from the solutions we've implemented working with family businesses over the past twenty-five-plus years.

We couple our academic, professional, and personal experiences as a father–son team running a business together to serve as an objective and neutral party providing customized and effective solutions to drive positive and lasting change. With the goal of building better alignment, communication, and relationships among all stakeholders, our flexible consulting process enables us to address the specific, unique challenges and opportunities of each family business.

THE PEER ALLIANCE
FORUMS FOR ENTERPRISING FAMILIES

The Peer Alliance is the leading peer forum group focused specifically on members of family enterprises who want to learn from the experiences of their peers to apply best practices and strategies for success in their own family enterprise. Forum is the most powerful solution to problems commonly affecting enterprising families. Why? Because forum members have been there before. They've lived many of the issues you are facing and can share knowledge, skill, and experience allowing you to drive better results in your family business.

Forum groups consist of noncompeting family enterprise stakeholders who meet quarterly for a full day of education and professionally facilitated confidential discussions. It's all about peer-to-peer learning and idea exchange. It's an investment in personal and professional development.

TAKE A HEALTH CHECK.

On our website, FamBizConsulting.com, we developed a "Family Business Health Check" designed to spark your reflection on the health of your family enterprise. (See also Addendum #17: Family Business Health Check.) Feel free to complete this form, and we would be pleased to talk with you about your results.

Visit FamBizConsulting.com to learn how we can help your family business, or simply drop us an email or give us a call to see if we might be able to help.

Transition Consulting Group, Ltd. | Framingham, MA
Palm Beach Gardens, FL | FamBizConsulting.com
info@FamBizConsulting.com | 508.875.7751